OPPOSING
VIEWPOINTS®
SERIES

Gambling

Other Books of Related Interest:

Opposing Viewpoints Series
Addiction
Alternative Lending
American Values
Debt
Unemployment

At Issue Series
Do Tax Breaks Benefit the Economy?
What Is the Impact of Tourism?

Current Controversies Series
Consumer Debt
The U.S. Economy

"Congress shall make no law ... abridging the freedom of speech, or of the press."

First Amendment to the US Constitution

The basic foundation of our democracy is the First Amendment guarantee of freedom of expression. The *Opposing Viewpoints* series is dedicated to the concept of this basic freedom and the idea that it is more important to practice it than to enshrine it.

OPPOSING VIEWPOINTS® SERIES

Gambling

Margaret Haerens, Book Editor

GREENHAVEN PRESS
A part of Gale, Cengage Learning

GALE
CENGAGE Learning˙

Detroit • New York • San Francisco • New Haven, Conn • Waterville, Maine • London

HV
6710
.G31416
2012

GALE
CENGAGE Learning

Elizabeth Des Chenes, *Managing Editor*

© 2012 Greenhaven Press, a part of Gale, Cengage Learning.

Gale and Greenhaven Press are registered trademarks used herein under license.

For more information, contact:
Greenhaven Press
27500 Drake Rd.
Farmington Hills, MI 48331-3535
Or you can visit our Internet site at gale.cengage.com

For product information and technology assistance, contact us at

Gale Customer Support, 1-800-877-4253
For permission to use material from this text or product, submit all requests online at www.cengage.com/permissions

Further permissions questions can be emailed to permissionrequest@cengage.com

Articles in Greenhaven Press anthologies are often edited for length to meet page requirements. In addition, original titles of these works are changed to clearly present the main thesis and to explicitly indicate the author's opinion. Every effort is made to ensure that Greenhaven Press accurately reflects the original intent of the authors. Every effort has been made to trace the owners of copyrighted material.

Cover Image Alhovik/Shutterstock.com

LIBRARY OF CONGRESS CATALOGING-IN-PUBLICATION DATA

Gambling / Margaret Haerens, book editor.
    p. cm. -- (Opposing viewpoints)
    Includes bibliographical references and index.
    ISBN 978-0-7377-5838-2 (hardcover) -- ISBN 978-0-7377-5839-9 (pbk.)
    1. Gambling--Social aspects. 2. Gambling--Government policy--United States.
    3. Internet gambling. I. Haerens, Margaret
    HV6710.G31416 2011
    363.4'20973--dc22
                                          2011008684

Printed in the United States of America
1 2 3 4 5 6 7 15 14 13 12 11

Contents

Chapter 2: What Are the Economic and Social Implications of Gambling?

Chapter 3: How Should the US Government Treat Online Gambling?

Chapter 4: What Are the Effects of Online Gambling?

Why Consider Opposing Viewpoints?

> "The only way in which a human being can make some approach to knowing the whole of a subject is by hearing what can be said about it by persons of every variety of opinion and studying all modes in which it can be looked at by every character of mind. No wise man ever acquired his wisdom in any mode but this."
>
> *John Stuart Mill*

In our media-intensive culture it is not difficult to find differing opinions. Thousands of newspapers and magazines and dozens of radio and television talk shows resound with differing points of view. The difficulty lies in deciding which opinion to agree with and which "experts" seem the most credible. The more inundated we become with differing opinions and claims, the more essential it is to hone critical reading and thinking skills to evaluate these ideas. Opposing Viewpoints books address this problem directly by presenting stimulating debates that can be used to enhance and teach these skills. The varied opinions contained in each book examine many different aspects of a single issue. While examining these conveniently edited opposing views, readers can develop critical thinking skills such as the ability to compare and contrast authors' credibility, facts, argumentation styles, use of persuasive techniques, and other stylistic tools. In short, the Opposing Viewpoints Series is an ideal way to attain the higher-level thinking and reading skills so essential in a culture of diverse and contradictory opinions.

In addition to providing a tool for critical thinking, *Opposing Viewpoints* books challenge readers to question their own strongly held opinions and assumptions. Most people form their opinions on the basis of upbringing, peer pressure, and personal, cultural, or professional bias. By reading carefully balanced opposing views, readers must directly confront new ideas as well as the opinions of those with whom they disagree. This is not to argue simplistically that everyone who reads opposing views will—or should—change his or her opinion. Instead, the series enhances readers' understanding of their own views by encouraging confrontation with opposing ideas. Careful examination of others' views can lead to the readers' understanding of the logical inconsistencies in their own opinions, perspective on why they hold an opinion, and the consideration of the possibility that their opinion requires further evaluation.

Evaluating Other Opinions

To ensure that this type of examination occurs, *Opposing Viewpoints* books present all types of opinions. Prominent spokespeople on different sides of each issue as well as well-known professionals from many disciplines challenge the reader. An additional goal of the series is to provide a forum for other, less known, or even unpopular viewpoints. The opinion of an ordinary person who has had to make the decision to cut off life support from a terminally ill relative, for example, may be just as valuable and provide just as much insight as a medical ethicist's professional opinion. The editors have two additional purposes in including these less known views. One, the editors encourage readers to respect others' opinions—even when not enhanced by professional credibility. It is only by reading or listening to and objectively evaluating others' ideas that one can determine whether they are worthy of consideration. Two, the inclusion of such viewpoints encourages the important critical thinking skill of objectively evaluating an author's credentials and bias. This evaluation will illuminate an author's reasons for taking a particular stance on an issue and will aid in readers' evaluation of the author's ideas.

It is our hope that these books will give readers a deeper understanding of the issues debated and an appreciation of the complexity of even seemingly simple issues when good and honest people disagree. This awareness is particularly important in a democratic society such as ours in which people enter into public debate to determine the common good. Those with whom one disagrees should not be regarded as enemies but rather as people whose views deserve careful examination and may shed light on one's own.

Thomas Jefferson once said that "difference of opinion leads to inquiry, and inquiry to truth." Jefferson, a broadly educated man, argued that "if a nation expects to be ignorant and free . . . it expects what never was and never will be." As individuals and as a nation, it is imperative that we consider the opinions of others and examine them with skill and discernment. The *Opposing Viewpoints* series is intended to help readers achieve this goal.

David L. Bender and Bruno Leone,
Founders

Introduction

"As the popularity of online gambling has grown, so too has the urge among some politicians and regulators who see it as a problem to 'do something' about it."

—*Michelle Minton,*
Competitive Enterprise Institute,
February 19, 2009

In December 2010 Nevada senator Harry Reid introduced a bill to legalize Internet poker in the United States. The bill would have overturned a 2006 law that bans financial institutions from processing online-gambling transactions. Critics of online gambling point to the fact that legalizing online gambling would directly benefit Reid's home state of Nevada, as gambling is Nevada's biggest industry, and legalization would benefit the gambling industry, which contributed money to Reid's 2010 reelection campaign. Other observers, however, ask why US companies shouldn't be able to get a piece of the estimated $5 billion annual revenue from the 10 million US consumers who now go to offshore casinos. Moreover, why shouldn't Americans be able to legally partake in online poker, betting, and casino games if that is what they want to do?

These questions have informed earlier debates about online gambling and the US legislature's attempts to grapple with this complicated and thorny issue. With the rise of the Internet in the 1990s came an explosion of online businesses trying to capitalize on the new technology. The gambling industry was no different; the first online gambling site was launched in August 1995. Today, more than two thousand gambling sites offer casino games, poker, lotteries, sports betting, and bingo. Members of the US Congress recognized the potential and the threat of online gambling early on and struggled with ways to deal with the growing popularity of such sites. An explicit ban on online gambling was unsuccessful because it would have a profound impact on a variety of interests, including Internet service providers, state governments, and different segments of the gaming industry, resulting in Congress looking for other ways to effectively ban the practice.

The US Justice Department in both the Bill Clinton and George W. Bush administrations declared that two older pieces of US legislation would be applicable to Internet gambling: the Interstate Wire Act of 1961, which prohibited gambling over the "wires"; and the Professional and Amateur Sports Protection Act of 1992 (PASPA), which banned sports betting in all states except those with preexisting operations (Nevada, Montana, Oregon, and Delaware). In the federal government's view, the Interstate Wire Act would apply to all forms of Internet gambling, making it illegal under existing law. In 2002 this view was found erroneous by the US Court of Appeals for the Fifth Circuit, which affirmed a lower court ruling that under the Interstate Wire Act online sports betting is illegal—but casino games are not.

In light of that court ruling, Congress went in a different direction. In 2006 it introduced legislation that would ban the use of credit cards and payment-processing systems for the purpose of illegal Internet gambling. The Unlawful Internet Gambling Enforcement Act (UIGEA) works to eliminate payment mechanisms used by offshore gambling websites, making it illegal for US banks, credit card companies, or other payment-processing businesses to collect on a debt from an Internet gambling website—thereby cutting off access to them for US gamblers. It was the first federal legislation restricting online gambling. As critics noted, however, the UIGEA does not clearly define what is illegal and what is legal, thereby keeping a gray area that many gambling operations continue to exploit.

Lawmakers have worked to end that exploitation. Some states have passed explicit bans on all Internet gambling. There are also laws against owning an online gambling operation, and no state licenses such operations. Many conservative commentators and politicians continued to express their vehement opposition to a practice they felt was immoral and preyed on American consumers. For them, federal and state governments had an obligation to protect their citizens from a predatory business. As Congressman Bob Goodlatte stated in his testimony during a 2007 hearing on Internet gambling, "Contrary to what many in the gambling community would lead you to believe, gambling is not a victimless activity. In fact, the negative consequences of online gambling can be more detrimental to the families and communities of addictive gamblers than if a bricks-and-mortar casino was built right next door."

In the late 2000s, however, the backlash to antigambling efforts gathered strength. Many libertarians, conservatives, and liberals argued that banning online gambling was an encroachment of civil liberties. Central to this perspective was the belief that individuals should have a right to spend their money in the way they please. As Congressman Barney Frank, chairman of the House Committee on Financial Services, contended during a hearing on Internet gambling in 2007, "in the end, adults ought to be able to decide for themselves how they will spend the money that they earn themselves, as long as it does not have an effect on others." Another congressman, Ron Paul, argued during that same hearing that choice was the mark of a free society: "Freedom of choice is important in a free society. Responsibility for improving one's behavior should be on the individual, the family, and the church and local community, not on the federal government. It hasn't worked before, and it probably won't ever work in the future."

The authors of the viewpoints featured in *Opposing Viewpoints: Gambling* explore the debate over gambling issues in the following chapters: How Should Gambling Be Treated?

What Are the Economic and Social Implications of Gambling? How Should the US Government Treat Online Gambling? and What Are the Effects of Online Gambling? The information presented in this volume provides insight into some of the recent controversies surrounding online gambling, thoroughbred horse racing, greyhound racing, and racinos—gambling facilities housed in racetracks—as well as other topics concerning the contentious issue of gambling.

 **OPPOSING VIEWPOINTS® SERIES**

How Should Gambling Be Treated?

Chapter Preface

On December 13, 2010, New Jersey lawmakers elected to allow voters to decide in the next statewide election whether sports betting should be allowed at New Jersey racetracks. Such a change would not be easy—it would involve changing the state constitution and finding a way around a federal ban on the practice. Yet these New Jersey lawmakers look to the practice of sports betting as a much-needed source of revenue and a way to open the door for sports betting in a struggling Atlantic City, one of America's premier gambling locations.

Sports betting involves placing a wager on the outcome of a college or professional sporting event, usually with a bookmaker or an Internet betting site. Wagering on sports is controversial; major amateur and professional sports leagues actively oppose the practice. They charge that sports betting would lead to a profound corruption of sports. College and professional players would be pressured to perform a certain way for bookies to make money, engaging in a practice known as "fixing" a game.

Fixing games is a staple of both amateur and professional sports. It has happened numerous times in American sports history; one of the most infamous examples is the fixing of the 1919 World Series. In that series, several players from the Chicago White Sox were paid by gamblers to purposely lose the world championship games against the Cincinnati Reds. After several more scandals in various sports, the federal government acted to strictly regulate and limit sports wagering to protect the integrity of college and professional sports. In 1992 the federal government passed the Professional and Amateur Sports Protection Act, which banned sports wagering business in all states except those with preexisting businesses— Nevada, Montana, Oregon, and Delaware.

Like the states that allow sports betting, New Jersey looks to the practice as a way to gain revenue. Experts estimate that New Jersey could see thousands of new jobs, $7 billion in annual gross gambling revenue, and up to $472 million in annual state gaming taxes if it becomes a leader in the industry. Lawmakers also look to sports betting as a way to save the state's racetracks, draw more celebrities and high rollers into the casinos, and attract more publicity to Atlantic City's struggling gambling entertainment businesses. New Jersey residents agree: a Fairleigh Dickinson University PublicMind poll found in April 2009 that 63 percent of New Jersey residents supported legalizing sports betting in Atlantic City and at horse racing tracks.

Yet the public also realizes that sports betting has inherent problems. Like college athletic associations and professional sports leagues, New Jersey residents are concerned that the practice threatens the integrity of both amateur and professional sports. In the same PublicMind poll, 54 percent of the New Jersey voters who opposed national legalized sports betting cited corruption of the game as their top concern about allowing the practice at New Jersey racetracks and Atlantic City casinos.

Atlantic City casinos also oppose legalizing sports betting. The city's casinos came out against allowing the practice because it would violate existing federal bans on sports and online betting and would primarily benefit offshore gambling websites and not New Jersey casinos.

The controversy over sports betting is one of the topics explored in the following chapter, which considers how policy makers should treat the issue of gambling. Other viewpoints debate whether horse racing and dog racing should be legal and whether gambling should be restricted.

> *"Instead of challenging citizens to save money and focusing on businesses that create new wealth instead of milking existing wealth, the government programme of predatory gambling does just the opposite."*

Gambling Must Be Restricted

Les Bernal

Les Bernal is the executive director of the antigambling Stop Predatory Gambling Foundation. In the following viewpoint, he contends that the American government has a responsibility to restrict gambling because it strips people of their freedom by making them gambling addicts. Bernal also argues that the financial and social costs of gambling make it a danger to the American people—and the American people must address the problem.

As you read, consider the following questions:

1. How many casinos are in the United States, according to the author?

2. According to a report mentioned in the viewpoint, what effect does predatory gambling have on state budget deficits?

3. How many electronic gambling machines are there in the United States?

A 49-year-old seventh-grade English teacher in New Hampshire was arrested earlier this year [2010] for robbing three banks. The description given by the banks was that of a short, middle-aged woman, wearing a heavy winter coat and scarf. She was unarmed and slipping tellers handwritten demands on envelopes. After being arrested and released on bail, she was ordered by a judge to attend Gamblers Anonymous. Police said she used the stolen money to gamble at the casinos in Connecticut.

How does a seventh-grade English teacher who appears as "a short, middle-aged woman, wearing a heavy winter coat and scarf" suddenly become a bank robber? Has such a bank robber ever before existed?

The government programme of casinos and lotteries is based on addicted or heavily indebted citizens just like this woman. Casinos like Harrah's make 90% of their gambling profits from the financial losses of 10% of their visitors, according to Christina Binkley's book, *Winner Takes All*. Lotteries collect 70% of their profits from the financial losses of 10% of their users, according to Matthew Sweeney's book, *The Lottery Wars*.

Myth of Personal Freedom

Commercial gambling promoters attempt to elude charges of exploitation by pleading it is a "voluntary" act, hiding behind well-intentioned people who argue the case for "personal freedom". But the business model for casinos and lotteries only works if our government takes away the freedom of millions of Americans. By definition, someone who is an addict or

Predatory Gambling Doubles Bankruptcy Rates

It takes three to five years for gamblers in a newly opened market to exhaust their resources. When addiction ripens in the market, so do the social costs. A study of all the casino counties in the nation confirmed personal bankruptcy rates are 100% higher in counties with casinos than in counties without casinos.

Stop Predatory Gambling Foundation,
"The Cost," 2010. http://stoppredatorygambling.org.

someone who is in deep financial debt is not free. We live in a country where everyone is considered equal. We do not have kings and queens. In America, all blood is royal. So how can the states actively promote a federal government programme that strips freedom from millions of citizens and renders them expendable?

"Foolishness with our own money should not be illegal," respond those like Radley Balko, as if the experience of the seventh-grade English teacher was a result of imprudence. Yet these expendable Americans not only lose their own cash, they also cost taxpayers a lot of extra money. In one of the only independent studies on the costs of predatory gambling, the New Hampshire Gaming Study Commission recently showed that taxpayers will need to fork out an additional $68m [million] in taxes to cover the social costs of one proposed casino, 24% more than the state government will receive in revenue. These numbers are for only one casino—there are now almost 900 casinos in America. It confirms a report by the [Nelson A.] Rockefeller Institute [of Government], a New York think tank, which found predatory gambling exacerbates state budget deficits over the long term. It also helps explain why the budgets of casino states like California, New York, Pennsylvania, Illinois and Nevada face enormous deficits.

Mr Balko and some others . . . draw a distinction between private for-profit gambling among individuals and government-run gambling programmes like casinos and lotteries. While I understand the argument, it does not reflect reality. Because the social costs associated with for-profit gambling are so significant, as shown by the New Hampshire study, the government will permit it only if it receives a large cut of the profits. That is why commercial gambling interests spend hundreds of millions of dollars promoting a bogus narrative declaring they represent the answer to the government's budget crisis.

US Government Promotes Gambling

It is likely Mr Balko would agree that there is a major difference between promoting gambling and prohibiting gambling. Today, the daily voice of government to most Americans— casino and lottery advertising—promotes gambling relentlessly. There are at least 800,000 electronic gambling machines spread all over the nation—one for every 395 Americans. Instant lottery scratch tickets, some worth up to $50, are being sold in tens of thousands of locations in cities and towns across the country. And now some in government are trying to bring casinos and lotteries into every home in America with a computer in the name of collecting more tax dollars. If this is considered an era of gambling prohibition by some, what would an era of legalisation look like?

In his opening remarks, the moderator observed that "people love to bet". Today, the government, by every measure, is exploiting this desire. Instead of challenging citizens to save money and focusing on businesses that create new wealth instead of milking existing wealth, the government programme of predatory gambling does just the opposite.

No issue better symbolises how the American government is broken. It is up to us to fix it.

"*[Risk taking] is the great engine of economic growth and the growth of risk industries—the stock market, venture capitalists and, yes, gambling—is evidence of that.*"

Gambling Should Not Be Restricted

Shikha Dalmia

Shikha Dalmia is a columnist at Forbes *and a senior policy analyst at the Reason Foundation. In the following viewpoint, she asserts that most of the charges made by antigambling crusaders are not backed up by factual evidence. Dalmia argues that antigambling crusaders are really risk averse and repulsed by the gambling ethos of risk and reward.*

As you read, consider the following questions:

1. What was the mentality of antigambling foes gathered at a National Coalition Against Legalized Gambling conference in October 2005?

2. According to a 1999 National Gambling Impact Study Commission report, what percentage of Americans have a gambling problem?

3. According to a study by Professor Jay Albanese, did white-collar crimes in the largest casino markets increase or decrease from 1988 to 1996?

Very rarely does reality supply scenarios that neatly capture every dimension of a social issue. But antigambling advocates always try to beat these odds.

Pick any article on the subject and it will invariably begin with a story that illustrates every possible ill associated with gambling: A happy man leading a normal life walks into a casino for the first time and—a few years later—he has lost his home, emptied his bank account, divorced his wife, sold his dog, embezzled money from his employer and is contemplating suicide to avoid a jail term.

Yet anecdotes about ruined losers are no more representative of the consequences of gambling than anecdotes about big jackpot winners.

The Fanaticism of Antigambling Crusaders

But the anecdotal methodology suits antigambling crusaders who regard any distinctions of degree or kind as subversive of their cause: Gambling is inherently wrong and, therefore, ought to be banned everywhere in all forms: state lottos, casinos, slot machines, race tracks and, their new bugaboo, Internet gambling.

That, at least, was the mentality of the antigambling foes gathered at a National Coalition Against Legalized Gambling conference in October [2005] in Washington, D.C., where speaker after speaker accused gambling of breeding exploitation, addiction, crime, suicide, homicide and divorce.

But is this hyperventilating justified?

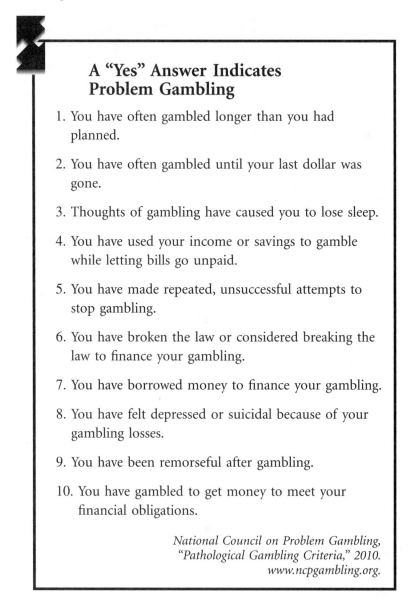

A "Yes" Answer Indicates Problem Gambling

1. You have often gambled longer than you had planned.

2. You have often gambled until your last dollar was gone.

3. Thoughts of gambling have caused you to lose sleep.

4. You have used your income or savings to gamble while letting bills go unpaid.

5. You have made repeated, unsuccessful attempts to stop gambling.

6. You have broken the law or considered breaking the law to finance your gambling.

7. You have borrowed money to finance your gambling.

8. You have felt depressed or suicidal because of your gambling losses.

9. You have been remorseful after gambling.

10. You have gambled to get money to meet your financial obligations.

National Council on Problem Gambling,
"Pathological Gambling Criteria," 2010.
www.ncpgambling.org.

Are Gamblers Exploited?

Take exploitation, for instance: Even the most enthusiastic gambling supporter would concede that there is an element of exploitation in state lottos. Having awarded themselves a monopoly over lottos, states have systematically raised ticket prices, reduced payouts and generally ripped off their customers, a big portion of whom tend to be poor.

On the other hand, casinos, where competition is fierce, treat their customers like kings, often showering them with no-strings-attached, all-paid-for trips with free tokens for any game of choice. You can't accuse them of exploitation. Right.

Wrong.

In the moral universe of gambling opponents, casinos' behavior is even more exploitative. It is designed to hook people on a product that, one speaker at the ... conference claimed, is "as addictive as cigarettes." What's more, according to another speaker, some people have a predisposition for gambling because their brains produce more dopamine and serotonin.

A single visit to the casino will turn these genetic suckers into permanent addicts and the casino freebies are all part of a plot to rope the dopes.

But the facts do not support these claims.

Examining the Data

Despite the growth of casinos, the number of problem gamblers has hardly budged: The first federal commission on gambling in the 1970s found that 0.77 percent of the U.S. population had a gambling disorder. Three decades later in 1999, the National Gambling Impact Study Commission reported that less than 1 percent of the adult U.S. population had gambling issues. Furthermore, the commission—which, by the way, is no friend of the gambling industry since it supported a moratorium on the expansion of legalized gambling—found no evidence that communities within driving distance of casinos experience a higher incidence of compulsive gambling than others.

But what about crime in casinos?

Is Gambling Dangerous?

It is indisputable that the entry of publicly traded companies whose shareholder profits depend on running a reputable business have radically cleaned up the casino industry, extricating it from the hands of Bugsy Segal–type mobsters.

But, gambling foes claim, casinos lead to more "violent crime, juvenile crime, drug- and alcohol-related crime, public corruption, domestic violence—including child abuse—and white-collar crime."

Potentially, every industry contributes to some kind of crime: bars, drunk driving; Hollywood movies, adultery, promiscuity and violence; Disney World, pickpockets. But the accusation that heavy losses by gambling addicts breeds white-collar crime such as embezzlement, forgery and fraud has gained much currency in the mainstream press in recent years.

However, the evidence for this is nonexistent as well.

The most comprehensive study examining the impact of casino gambling on white-collar crime, conducted by Professor Jay Albanese, a professor of criminal justice at Virginia Commonwealth University found a net decrease in arrests for white-collar crimes in the largest casino markets from 1988 to 1996.

But such scientific findings don't quell the fears of gambling opponents, they only heighten them. Why? Is it out of some deep-seated fear about people exposing themselves to potential ruin?

The Fear of Winning

Actually, it is the opposite: It is fear of people winning that feeds this moral angst.

When people gamble and win they undercut the old-fashioned virtues of frugality, prudence and hard work—all things that in the puritan mind are necessary for economic growth.

These virtues are not obsolete. But they were never the sole drivers of the capitalist economy. Entrepreneurship and risk taking were also essential and in the information economy—in which ideas and innovation are the main drivers—they are more essential than ever.

Moreover, not only does a modern, dynamic economy require risk, it lowers the disincentive to risk. It releases capital and opportunities, making it easier for people who lose fortunes to bounce back quickly. In effect, it makes risk less risky.

In the end, it is not the social effects but the ethos of gambling that opponents raised in a more risk-averse, moral universe hate. Yet risk taking is the great engine of economic growth and the growth of risk industries—the stock market, venture capitalists and, yes, gambling—is evidence of that.

This is why risk takers—who are gamblers—will inherit the future.

You can bet on it.

"People are responsible for the consequences of their bad habits."

Government Should Not Be Hypocritical on the Gambling Issue

John Stossel

John Stossel is an author, journalist, and syndicated columnist. In the following viewpoint, he maintains that the federal government should not be treating Americans like children—if they want to gamble, they should be allowed to do so if they are willing to deal with the consequences. Stossel points out that while government bans many forms of gambling, most state governments run lotteries.

As you read, consider the following questions:

1. Why does the author believe that the 1999 National Gambling Impact Study Commission report distorts the number of Americans with a gambling problem?

2. How much do state lotteries take out of each bet compared to casinos?

3. How much does Stossel estimate the United States has lost by forcing Internet gambling offshore?

Some of us like to gamble. Americans bet a hundred million dollars every day, and that's just at legal places like Las Vegas and Indian reservations. Much more is bet illegally.

So authorities crack down. They raided a VFW [Veterans of Foreign Wars] branch that ran a poker game for charity. They ban lotteries, political futures markets and sports betting. They raid truck stops to confiscate video poker machines. Why?

Chad Hills of Focus on the Family says: "These machines have been shown to be extremely addictive. That's a huge concern, primarily for kids, because it's hard to keep them away."

Well, I certainly agree kids shouldn't gamble, and some people do wreck their lives. But why can't adults be left to do what we want to do?

Prohibition Does Not Work

Hills and Sen. Jon Kyl, R-Ariz., both eager to ban gambling, talk about "addiction" leading to bankruptcy, crime and suicide.

I'm skeptical. People are responsible for the consequences of their bad habits. I thought Focus on the Family and conservatives like Kyl believed in self-responsibility.

Professional poker player Andy Bloch points out that, legal or not, gambling already goes on everywhere. Prohibition doesn't rid society of an activity. It drives it underground, where it's less visible and less subject to respectable social conventions.

As for people getting into trouble, Bloch noted that after online gaming was legalized in the United Kingdom, "they found that there was no significant increase in the number of problem gamblers."

US States with State Lotteries

■ With state lotteries   ■ Without state lotteries

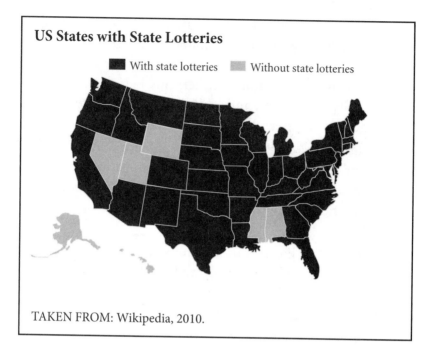

TAKEN FROM: Wikipedia, 2010.

People Want to Gamble

Hills, on the other hand, claims that a 2006 anti-Internet gaming law reduced gambling. "People say this drives gambling underground," he added. "I'm like, good, drive it underground."

I point out that people still find the gambling sites.

"But it makes it extremely difficult. You have to be fairly desperate to do it."

I doubt that anyone who wants to gamble illegally has trouble doing it. And let's not forget the official corruption that black markets encourage. Law enforcement people take bribes to look the other way. It's an old story.

Hills claims that the 1999 National Gambling Impact Study [Commission report] concluded that 15 million Americans are problem and pathological gamblers. But like many people who want to ban things, he distorts the data. The study's 15 million "problem gamblers" included people who might get in trouble.

"Ninety-nine percent of the American public has no problem with gambling," Bloch says. "They should have the freedom to gamble if they want to gamble online. There is no casino that is being forced into people's homes."

Countering the Moral Argument

By the way, Hills said he'd oppose legal gambling even if it weren't associated with wrecked lives. Why? "Gambling is the art and the science of deception that feeds on the exploitation of human weakness for the sole purpose of monetary gain."

To that, I say, so what? Will they ban the stock market next? Filmmaking is the art and science of deception. Poker is just a game where deception and bluffing are the skills.

For self-responsible adults, gambling can be fun and harmless. A free country is supposed to treats adults as though we are self-responsible. Government should let us learn from our mistakes rather than treat us like children.

The Government Is Hypocritical

Despicably, while government outlaws private gambling (at least that which competes with the well-connected casino interests), it runs its own gambling operations: state lotteries. And what a scam they are! States offer terrible odds. The evil casinos take about 1.4 percent of each bet at the craps table. State lotteries take 50 percent of each bet. Compounding the damage, states spend tax money to promote their lotteries to the poor, who are led to believe that the lottery, rather than hard work, is the route to becoming millionaires. Rich people buy few tickets.

So governments push their own inferior games while outlawing better ones run by private business. That's insane. People gamble anyway, criminals get involved, and by forcing Internet gambling offshore, America loses a $12 billion industry.

In *On Liberty*, John Stuart Mill wrote, "Over himself and over his own body and mind, the individual is sovereign."

Sovereign. Hear that, busybody politicians?

"There is too much hypocrisy and hyperbole around sports and how it builds character and is bedrock for young people. It is just a business. That's all."

Sports Betting Should Be Legal

Evan Weiner

Evan Weiner is a journalist, author, and TV commentator. In the following viewpoint, he contends that it is time to legalize sports betting because the fearmongering from professional sports leagues about the dangers of gambling is hypocritical and false. Weiner points out that sports betting can be a lucrative revenue stream for cash-strapped local and state governments.

As you read, consider the following questions:

1. Where are sports books legal in the United States, according to Weiner?

2. According to the viewpoint, in what states is sports wagering legal?

3. Why does the author believe that the integrity argument doesn't hold true anymore when it comes to legalizing sports betting?

In the capital city of the British Crown colony of Bermuda, Hamilton, there is a rather non-descript store located beneath the Little Theater on Queen Street. There are two signs in front of the property, one in green and the other in white, which describe the place.

"Sea Horses—Live English and U.S. Horse Racing, International Sports Betting, Open Monday–Saturday."

Sea Horses Bookmakers is a Bermuda-owned company that is licensed by the Bermuda government and Americans sitting at home can use their computers to bet on American pro and college sports events. Ironically enough, there is no casino gambling on the Bermuda islands.

The Sea Horses betting parlor is around the corner from the Hamilton City Hall and is about two blocks up from the very upscale waterfront that includes the U.K.'s Marks & Spencer. The sports book is the kind of place that exists in the United Kingdom but not in the United States except in Las Vegas and Dover, Delaware. Inside a cutaway in a building under the Little Theater, on the left side is Sea Horses, a place that will never be confused for Las Vegas or Dover or what might be a sports book in an Atlantic City casino.

Inside the Betting Parlor

There are Venetian blinds on the door and window of the store so you cannot look in. Once inside, the room is small and drab with a bank of lower-end televisions showing horse races from various tracks around the world and English football. The dozen or so men, it was all men, were going through racing forms, American football games tout sheets, which resembled betting sheets that were used at high schools in the 1970s around the U.S. that looked like they came straight out of [a] mimeograph machine. The games were listed along with game times, all the game times were listed in Atlantic Daylight Time, so all of the NBC Sunday night NFL games don't start until 9:30 locally. The English Premiership Games start in the afternoon or in the morning with the four-hour time difference between Bermuda and the U.K. The bettors don't care about times though.

The English football sheets were slick.

The Football Pools

"The Football Pools" had all sorts of betting schemes. But there was something striking about the Football Pools. In the middle of the page there was a logo of the English Premier League. The Premiership is an official licensee of the Football Pools, and another football group, the Scottish Premier League, is an official partner of the Football Pools.

The Football Pools happens to be "The Official Pools Partner of the Professional Football Leagues."

Ties Between American Sports and Gambling

Contrast the U.K. and the various football associations globally attitude toward sports betting with that of the United States. Officials connected with the biggest global sport are partners in gambling. National Basketball Association [NBA] Commissioner David Stern has thought about gambling proceeds as a possible revenue source for his league.

Stern's Women's National Basketball Association [WNBA] has the Connecticut Sun franchise. That team is owned by the Mohegan Sun casino. LeBron James may have not cared for his former boss—the Cleveland Cavaliers owner Dan Gilbert—but Gilbert will own the casino that is being built near the Cavaliers arena in downtown Cleveland.

The owner of the National Hockey League's Detroit Red Wings and Major League Baseball's Detroit Tigers has a stake in a casino. Mike Ilitch technically doesn't own the gambling hall in Detroit, his wife Marian does along with other Ilitch family members. The Ilitch family is interested in bringing a casino to Hawaii and Long Island.

The National Hockey League took a cut from the Alberta hockey lottery and has given some of the Alberta lottery money to the Canada province's two franchises in Calgary and Edmonton. Some casino money in Pittsburgh has been thrown into a newly opened arena in that city which houses the Pittsburgh Penguins.

Sports franchises in all sports in North America, even the National Football League, have agreements with casinos and state lotteries. The New York Giants partnered with Connecticut in 2009 on a state lottery promotion.

Drawing Lines

When gambling suits sports owners, they will embrace the revenues that they derive from slapping a team's logo on a scratch-off ticket. But there is still a ceiling on what betting is acceptable and sports books in casinos are not what the owners want and since a good many owners are also one of the powers behind politics, politicians stay away from legalizing betting on pro sports (and colleges) in the United States.

In the 1970s, Major League Baseball Commissioner [Bowie Kuhn] "suspended" Mickey Mantle and Willie Mays for being casino gamblers. Kuhn was worried about the integrity of the game. American sports has never embraced legal gambling because of "integrity" issues and having games fixed. But gambling is widespread across the country and there is legal sports wagering in Nevada, Oregon, Montana and Delaware.

In the 1990s, New Jersey politicians wanted to put a sports book in Atlantic City. Stern was among the sports industry leaders to lobby Trenton officials to give up their foolish thought. But Stern has a casino partner in the WNBA and he

What Americans Spend on Sports Betting

A recent federal study on gaming in the U.S. indicated that "there was up to $380 billion a year bet in this country on sports, of which only one percent is legally bet," said Frank Fahrenkopf, who used to run the Republican Party and is now gambling's top lobbyist.

Caitlin A. Johnson,
"Is Gambling in America's National DNA?"
CBSNews.com, February 4, 2007. www.cbsnews.com.

absolutely knows that NBA games are on legal betting sheets in Hamilton and other places around the world including Las Vegas.

In 2009, the National Collegiate Athletic Association [NCAA] and the National Football League [NFL] effectively stopped the establishment of a sports book in Dover Downs and two other spots in Delaware. There is NFL football parlay betting at Dover Downs and in Delaware.

Sports Leagues Flex Their Power

Sports leagues have blocked sports betting in the United States by convincing politicians outside of Delaware, Montana, Nevada and Oregon about the evils of betting. In 1992, the Professional and Amateur Sports Protection Act allowed just four states to have sports books with New Jersey actually qualifying as a fifth state if the New Jersey legislature passed a measure allowing a sports book because there was gambling in Atlantic City.

New Jersey lawmakers failed to pass a bill.

There are a lot of evils associated with gambling and gambling in many areas of the United States is being used as a revenue stream to help municipalities who are suffering revenue shortfalls as a way to help balance budgets. Gambling establishments also remind people in some form or another to be thoughtful about gambling since gambling addictions can cause massive problems in the proverbial cover yourself by issuing a warning that gambling can be self-destructive.

The standard bred horse racing industry in the United States would probably be close to dead without video slot machines inside racetracks. New York State has been playing around for years with establishing a casino at Aqueduct in Queens in an effort to keep thoroughbred racing alive.

In New Jersey, there are all sorts of proposals flying around to bolster Atlantic City and keep the state's horse tracks alive. But no one wants to wade into the let's legalize gambling on college and pro sports on a national scale even though gambling is out there.

The Truth About Pro Sports

Here's a truth about pro sports: It is not a sacred cow that needs to be treated with kid gloves. It is a business and people bet on pro sports. The whitewashing of pro football includes not saying much officially about point spreads. But as Vince McMahon pointed out in 2000, the biggest building block in his plan to build a football league 11 years ago was getting a Las Vegas line. McMahon ultimately failed because of stupid business practices with the XFL. The point spread and the over-under betting has given football fans an interactive experience for decades, long before the term interactive was invented.

The NCAA men's college basketball tournament is all about "brackets" which really is a code word for betting. Politicians don't want legalized betting on college games for integrity reasons. There have been college basketball betting scandals without legal betting.

So that excuse doesn't wash.

In the pro sports, baseball has worried about fixed games for nearly a century and hired Judge Kenesaw Mountain Landis as commissioner to clean up the game in the wake of the 1919 Chicago White Sox World Series gambling scandal. But there is a hollow ring to the integrity of the baseball issue when the game is closely scrutinized with owners' collusion in the 1980s and the use of banned substances by players in the 1990s. Baseball is not as pure as Caesar's wife as baseball writers probably could attest if they wanted to break baseball's unwritten code of what happens in the clubhouse stays in the clubhouse.

Time to Face the Truth

There are a lot of "Sea Horses" around the world complete with a website where betting can be found. Betting on professional sports is no big deal in Bermuda, the U.K. and other countries. There are sports betting parlors in various parts of the world outside the United States that are in business thanks to professional leagues. Integrity issues disappeared a long time ago in professional sports and the moralists who are disguised as politicians who think of betting as a scourge against sports need to explain . . . how there are dozens of ways you can spend money on state-based lottery games. Gambling has been a way of generating revenues for states for more than four decades around America.

Politicians might as well go all the way and approve full sports gambling in Atlantic City, Dover and other places. Sports is only sports, an entertainment forum. It's really nothing all that important in terms of lasting culture and legalized betting on sports should be viewed as just another taxation method that brings money into municipal coffers. There is too much hypocrisy and hyperbole around sports and how it builds character and is bedrock for young people. It is just a business. That's all. If people want to bet on sports, which they do, let them go to a casino showroom. What is the big

deal? People are going to bet anyway, whether it is in a color-
ful setting and casinos tend to build the illusion of a setting of
glamour or a small, dully painted square room which looks a
little worn around the walls with a cashier's booth tucked un-
derneath a theatre in a capital of a British colony.

"Everything is politics, it would seem. But complicated legislative loopholes aside, basing entire economies—and California's alone is the sixth largest in the entire world—on games of chance is quite the risky proposition itself."

States Rush to Legalize Sports Betting and Expand Gambling for Revenue

Diane M. Grassi

Diane M. Grassi is an investigative journalist. In the following viewpoint, she observes that sports betting is not the recession-proof industry that many cash-strapped states think it is. Grassi argues that legislators are viewing sports betting as a quick fix to state and local financial deficits and are not taking into account the troubled financial status of sports wagering in the past few years.

As you read, consider the following questions:

1. How much was wagered on the 2010 Super Bowl with Nevada sports books, according to the viewpoint?

2. Which states are proposing some form of sports betting?

3. How much in revenues does the Native American community receive every year, as stated by Grassi?

With the meltdown of the global economy over the past 2 years, multinational brokerage firms and trusted financial institutions bore the brunt of accusations of *gambling* away the financial health and futures of investors, primarily through the sale of toxic mortgages with credit default swaps as the vehicle in doing so.

Yet, it is the mainstreaming of gambling on many levels that has created a culture whereby it has become an acceptable norm for not only corporations but governments in the United States, on both the federal and state levels, to literally invest in the gambling industry, with the recession as the excuse for its necessity.

Yet, for years prior to the current recession, brokerage firms such as Goldman Sachs, Merrill Lynch and Fidelity Investments were already investing their clients' stocks and mutual fund portfolios, in financing offshore casinos.

The question remains as to whether they skirted U.S. federal law, which prohibits offshore online gambling for Americans, as well as to whether they made reliable investments on behalf of their clients, many of whom remain unaware that such financial instruments are involved in such volatile industries. So, Wall Street was already in on the game.

Looking for That Magic Bullet

Fast forward to 2010, where many U.S. states are on the precipice of bankruptcy and are desperate for that magic bullet to increase tax revenues without continually cutting services for their already over-taxed residents. And to that end, many state governors and state legislators are clamoring to push through laws in anticipation of overturning the federal law in place, prohibiting sports betting on both professional and amateur sports, otherwise known as the Professional and Amateur Sports Protection Act of 1992 (28 U.S.C. 3701) (PASPA).

To wit, the state legislature of New Jersey passed State Resolution No. 19 on January 12, 2010, which authorizes its President of the Senate to "take legal action concerning certain federal legislation prohibiting sports betting." It would repeal the federal ban on sports betting, in all other U.S. states, with the exception of Nevada, Delaware, Oregon and Montana, already permitted to offer parlay-type sports betting. Nevada, however, exclusively enjoys all types of sports betting, statewide, on any professional or amateur sports games, in any capacity.

Basically, New Jersey, and specifically Senator Raymond Lesniak, who originally launched a lawsuit on his own in March 2009 against the federal government, claims that the 1992 law violates the 10th and 14th Amendments to the U.S. Constitution, in that "it establishes a selective prohibition on sports betting in the U.S." The argument is that it violates the 10th Amendment to the United States Constitution by regulating a matter that is reserved to the states. And that it violates the 14th Amendment to the United States Constitution by being unconstitutionally discriminatory against the plaintiffs and the people of the state of New Jersey.

Lesniak's case presently resides in the U.S District Court, District of New Jersey, seeking declaratory relief. But the upshot is that New Jersey believes that it "would benefit significantly from lifting the federal ban and legalizing sports betting in this state, as increased revenues would be generated and numerous jobs would be created for New Jersey residents as a result of sports betting activities at Atlantic City casinos and New Jersey's racetracks, further enhancing tourism and economic growth," according to Resolution No. 19.

Is It Time to Legalize Sports Betting?

Prior to PASPA, the [Interstate] Wire Act was enacted in 1961. It was intended exclusively for prohibiting the placement of bets by telephone to bookmakers for sporting events, and was largely put in place by then U.S. attorney general Robert F. Kennedy in order to discourage organized crime and bookmaking. But gaming and its technology has come light-years since 1961, and it would appear that the Wire Act's shelf life has thus expired.

Meanwhile, in the U.S. Congress, House Representative Barney Frank (D-MA), chairman of the House Financial Services Committee, has promoted a federal resolution to legalize and regulate the Internet gambling industry in the U.S. (H.R. 2667). That proposal falls on the heels of the Unlawful Internet Gambling Enforcement Act of 2006 (UIGEA). It proscribes that offshore Internet gambling is a violation of federal law.

Furthermore, legislation was passed by the New Jersey legislature in its state Senate to amend the New Jersey State Constitution, allowing legalized sports betting, which the New Jersey voters would ultimately vote on in a referendum as early as November 2010.

But this constant back and forth between drafting new law and upholding existing legislation on a federal level to regulate gaming, runs in direct conflict with those states introducing new laws, geared to open up the flood gates for a variety of legalized gaming platforms, including sports betting. In addition, the National Indian Gaming Association, with respect to state Indian gaming contracts, originally authorized by the U.S. federal government, presents other conflicts on both state and federal levels.

What About Non-Gamblers?

Therefore, with the rights of gamblers continually in flux, the question must be asked what about the rights of non-gamblers and the resources that will be expended towards the downside that accompanies a gambling culture, upon which states will necessarily become dependent?

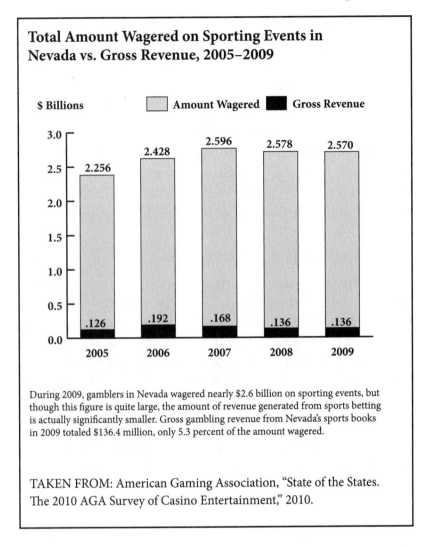

Total Amount Wagered on Sporting Events in Nevada vs. Gross Revenue, 2005–2009

During 2009, gamblers in Nevada wagered nearly $2.6 billion on sporting events, but though this figure is quite large, the amount of revenue generated from sports betting is actually significantly smaller. Gross gambling revenue from Nevada's sports books in 2009 totaled $136.4 million, only 5.3 percent of the amount wagered.

TAKEN FROM: American Gaming Association, "State of the States. The 2010 AGA Survey of Casino Entertainment," 2010.

In the state of Nevada alone, with unemployment approaching 23%, for those presently receiving extended unemployment benefits as well as those no longer receiving such benefits, it is the gaming industry specifically that is responsible for such a jobs freefall which accompanies a nearly $1 billion state budget shortfall. Add to that the highest mortgage foreclosure rates in the entire U.S. and there arises a recipe for disaster.

And as gaming drives all other industry including construction, conventions and tourism, primarily in Las Vegas, it would make one wonder what other state officials are thinking when gaming revenues in Las Vegas went down over 20% between 2008 and 2009, and it has yet to come out of its funk.

Las Vegas Strip properties' construction is at a virtual standstill with over-leveraged multinational conglomerates also reeling from the worldwide mortgage crisis. It appears that it was not only the little guys at the slot machines who gambled with their fortunes over the past few years.

Sports Betting Is a Panacea

With respect to sports betting on the National Football League's (NFL's) Super Bowl, Las Vegas betting revenues for the past 2 seasons of 2008 and 2009 were down considerably from years past. Nevada casino sports books in 2008 lost $2.6 million on the Super Bowl and in 2010 a total of $82.7 million was wagered with a net gain of only $179,000.00 more for casino sports books than in 2009. In contrast, $94.6 million was wagered in 2006, prior to the recession.

Yet, New Jersey is convinced and presupposes that sports wagering will generate hundreds of millions of dollars in state revenue over the course of a 5-year period, for its state alone. And it remains dedicated to also expand casino gambling in spite of its own realized massive decline in profits over the past 2 years.

But the state of New Jersey is hardly alone in its desire to gamble on gambling with many states introducing legislation and campaigning for both intrastate and interstate forms of gambling, both online and throughout casinos and racetrack locales throughout the U.S.

Currently, 48 states enjoy some form of legalized gambling and/or state lotteries, with the exception of Hawaii and Utah which do not presently permit any type of gambling, wagering or lotteries. However, Hawaii is presently weighing legislation for a stand-alone casino in Waikiki.

States in addition to New Jersey proposing sports betting and some type of expansion of casino gambling, including online gaming, with some states already preparing such legislation regarding sports betting in the event that PASPA is overturned includes: Iowa, Delaware, Massachusetts, California, Texas, Alabama, Missouri, Georgia, Florida, Pennsylvania, Indiana, Maine, New Hampshire, Connecticut, Michigan, Kentucky, Illinois, among others.

The Delaware Situation

In the case of Delaware, it won the right in 2009 to offer 3-game parlay style sports betting at its 3 racetracks or racinos [racetracks at which slot machines are available] for NFL games only, as states that previously offered lottery style or legalized sports betting from 1976–1990 were exempt from PASPA. Yet, after its well-fought challenge in federal court in 2009 for Delaware to be permitted to bet on all professional sports à la Las Vegas style without restrictions, it was defeated. But Delaware has not yet given up its fight and its case has been appealed to the U.S. Supreme Court.

The Iowa Situation

Iowa is also leading the charge in crafting legislation to allow legalized sports betting. However, Iowa State Senator Jerry Behn (R-Boone) thinks that gambling is a "tax on the people who can afford it the least." Yet, his colleague, State Senator Jack Kibbie (D-Emmetsburg) on betting on professional sports says, "People say I would love to do what they can do in Las Vegas."

Perhaps those with the same sentiments as those of Senator Kibbie will not be so game, so to speak, when there remains little discretionary income for such sin taxes to generate anticipated windfall profits.

California's New Plan

With respect to California's new plan there comes an additional rub. It plans to introduce an online gaming network. Yet, it potentially could be in violation of Indian gaming licenses or compact agreements that California entered into in 1999 with Native American tribes in its state. The compacts gave the tribes exclusive rights to any gambling that involved *gaming devices* including slot machines, roulette tables and video poker machines, etc.

Furthermore, it took 5 years for California to get the tribes to honor the payment of taxes due to the state of California by virtue of the compacts. The tribes withheld tax payments until 2004. However, the state of California still gives such exclusive rights to the Indian tribes through 2030, which remains a binding agreement to date.

Now, the California tribes have threatened to once again withhold paying the government of California its share of taxes due for gaming revenues, should California proceed with its online poker network plans. The state's position is that the compacts do not include poker and cover only games of chance. Yet, the tribal councils deem gaming devices to include computers used for online gaming, and thus negating California's plan.

Such a dustup could resonate through the Native American community, with its 442 tribal casinos operated by 237 tribal governments and Alaska native villages in 28 states. Revenues translate into a nearly $30 billion a year industry for them.

And Congressman Frank's legislation to regulate Internet poker would also be a direct threat to Indian gaming casinos, unless the Indian Gaming Regulatory Act of 1988 is somehow amended.

Ideally, California wants its poker network to go nationwide, raising revenues by ultimately licensing interstate networks and thereby generating additional profits through the ownership of such various licenses between states. The hope is that it could eventually trump PASPA.

Gambling Is Not the Answer

Everything is politics, it would seem. But complicated legislative loopholes aside, basing entire economies—and California's alone is the sixth largest in the entire world—on games of chance is quite the risky proposition itself.

And how taxpayers can be expected to trust their state governments to invest in struggling enterprises, already in the red, in order to prop up their cash-strapped states, many nearing junk-bond status due to irresponsible governing, remains the $64,000.00 question.

[There was a] time when Vegas thought gambling was recession proof. And there should be little doubt that Las Vegas now serves as the poster child for that which results when gamblers stop gambling and traveling to destination resorts.

And for public officials to abandon all reason and principles, looking for a quick fix, rather than by relying upon ingenuity for the creation of jobs and revenue outside of the gambling sector, could very well come back to bite them, in the end.

> "While there are some owners who care for their dogs and only raise and race a few greyhounds, the majority of owners treat their dogs as if they are solely monetary commodities."

Dog Racing Should Be Banned

Amy Pedigo

Amy Pedigo is a staff columnist for the UAB Kaleidoscope, *the newspaper for the University of Alabama at Birmingham. In the following viewpoint, she finds it absurd that the United States still breeds greyhounds for sport. Pedigo argues that this leads to excessive breeding, wanton neglect, and cruelty to greyhounds who do not excel on the racetrack.*

As you read, consider the following questions:

1. What happens to greyhounds after their racing careers are over, according to the author?

2. How are ex-racing greyhounds used at Auburn University?

3. What happens to losing dogs after races in third world countries, according to Pedigo?

Each year, thousands of greyhounds are euthanized after their racing careers are over. Deemed useless by many owners, the dogs who no longer measure up are cast aside.

While there are some owners who care for their dogs and only raise and race a few greyhounds, the majority of owners treat their dogs as if they are solely monetary commodities.

At Auburn, ex-racers are received as lab animals. Unfortunately for greyhounds, they have extremely docile dispositions when not on the track. When the dogs arrive at the university, they are either subjected to medical research or used in labs for dissections.

Though we do need medical advancements and practice for our nation's upcoming doctors and veterinarians, it need not be a factor in the propitiation in the racing industry.

One suggestion that comes off the top of my head would be to use the animals from our humane societies that have not been able to find homes. They are the result of society's inability to keep the animal population under control. Greyhound overpopulation is a pandemic that has a simple solution: Stop purposely overbreeding these animals.

Racing Dogs Live Bleak Lives

Luckily, there are many advocates for racing greyhounds. Birmingham is the home of a few rescue groups where retired dogs are placed in loving homes. But this is not enough. There is still senseless killing of dogs each year. Some live a "good, long life" of four or five years racing, others live only one or two years because they cannot make it past training, and yet others still are killed as puppies because they are simply not needed.

And as for the dogs who do prove to be fast enough to live, many are subjected to overcrowding in kennels (which leads to needless fights among some males), putrid Grade D meat as food, and often poor medical care, if any is administered at all.

Most Recent States to Ban Dog Racing

Maine (1993), Virginia (1995), Vermont (1995), Idaho (1996), Washington (1996), Nevada (1997), North Carolina (1998), Pennsylvania (2004), Massachusetts (2008, effective 2010), Rhode Island (2010) and New Hampshire (2010) are the most recent states to make dog racing illegal. The United States territory of Guam also outlawed commercial dog racing in 2010.

Grey2K USA,
"Fact Sheet: Greyhound Racing in the United States,"
Grey2KUSA.org, 2010. www.grey2kusa.org.

In third world countries, it is the norm to torture the dogs who are "losers" after races for cheap entertainment.

Often it is more cost effective to hang dogs in order to save the cost of a bullet or euthanasia drugs. The ropes can be used multiple times, not just once.

It has been a long while since the majority of the human race depended on dogs to help them hunt and catch food. So, the use for breeding dogs for the purpose of speed seems asinine. We are intelligent enough to find other means of occupying our time and spending our money in the pursuit of leisure. Yet, greyhound racing continues.

I ask: Why? Why do we endorse a pastime that is blatantly cruel? Legislators make efforts to control dog-fighting rings, calling them "inhumane." Why isn't this rationale applied to greyhound racing?

> *"The precedent set by banning an activity based on a limited perception that it is distasteful or repugnant is a far bigger risk for Massachusetts than the perpetuation of a sport that brings a sizable contingent of residents both enjoyment and employment."*

Dog Racing Should Not Be Banned

Harvard Crimson

The Harvard Crimson *is Harvard University's student newspaper. In the following viewpoint, the editorial writers urge voters to vote against the 2008 ballot Question 3 in Massachusetts, in favor of banning gambling on dog races in the state. The authors maintain that dog racing is closely and effectively regulated to protect the racing dogs and that opposition to the practice is grounded in classism rather than altruism.*

As you read, consider the following questions:

1. According to the Massachusetts Animal Interest Coalition, what is the fatality rate for the state's racing dogs?

2. How have the state's two dog tracks done in the past five years?

3. How many states permit dog racing, according to the authors?

The website of the Massachusetts Animal Interest Coalition (MAIC), a group established to oppose the passage of ballot Question 3—which would ban gambling on dog races across the state—presents a number of arguments against the initiative. It reminds readers of the thousands of jobs tied to dog racing within state borders, disputes the claim that dogs are mistreated under current sport regulations and cites a rate of fatality below one percent for the state's 2,066 racing greyhounds in the past calendar year [2008]. With a few exceptions, the many arguments advanced by MAIC against Question 3 are compelling ones.

More convincing, though, is the argument they don't make. MAIC's opponent, the group known as Grey2K [USA] responsible for supporting the ballot initiative, notes on their website that in Massachusetts, dog racing is already ceasing to be a real concern. At the state's two dog tracks, they observe, gambling revenues have dropped 65 and 37 percent in the last five years. In Revere, where one of those tracks is located, city officials are beginning the process of foreclosure: The management of Wonderland Greyhound Park has evidently failed to pay almost $790,000 in taxes since 2006.

Let Dog Racing Die on Its Own

Greyhound racing may die a death in Massachusetts, perhaps very soon. But there is no evidence that hastening its decline by coercive state intervention is the ideal, let alone a necessary, way to facilitate that decline. What is troubling about Question 3 is not the intention that guides its supporters, but rather the philosophy and predisposition that govern its practical form.

Massachusetts is one of just 16 states to permit dog racing inside its borders, but it does so with a healthy dose of oversight. For example, since 2001, state law has mandated that a veterinarian be on duty to examine greyhounds before and after each race, that dog droppings must be removed daily from the kennel area, and that the state racing commission should address every complaint of greyhound abuse. Between 2005 and 2006, just 0.15 percent of this state's racing dogs left the track with an injury—a proportion more than ten times smaller than were injured in girls high school softball in the same year.

Opponents of Dog Racing Are Classist

With this environment in mind, the proponent arguments for Question 3 seem grounded more clearly in classism than altruism. Dog racing—its once-pernicious impact minimized by the aforementioned regulation and adoption programs—remains entangled in a network of negative connotations, some of which have been exploited to advance Question 3 and other measures like it in the past. In reality, the practice has become no more detrimental or exploitative than thoroughbred racing or many other professional sports. The precedent set by banning an activity based on a limited perception that it is distasteful or repugnant is a far bigger risk for Massachusetts than the perpetuation of a sport that brings a sizable contingent of residents both enjoyment and employment.

Massachusetts voters should appreciate our right to submit ballot questions to change the way our state is run, and Question 3's proposed ban is a matter for legitimate discussion. We must, however, also take care to wield that power carefully—a responsibility that makes this particular initiative seem hasty and unjustified. Next Tuesday, we must allow prudence to trump perpetual intervention, and trust all of our citizens to make responsible decisions about their leisure time.

If, in coming years, state residents vote definitively against dog racing with their wallets—as they seem to be doing already—then the matter will be settled. Until then, better to let sleeping dogs lie—or racing dogs run.

"Commentators warn that if some such adjustments do not decrease the fatalities in racing, a sport that has already been fading in public enthusiasm could find itself in dire jeopardy even without laws bringing it to an end, and I suspect that's true."

Horse Racing Should Be Reformed

Jay Ambrose

Jay Ambrose is a newspaper editor and columnist. In the following viewpoint, he defends the sport of horse racing, asserting that thoroughbred horses are bred to race and receive better care than those that don't race. Ambrose admits that difficult and essential reforms are necessary to the sport to lessen horse injuries and fatalities, yet the American people should accept that an element of risk exists in every physical activity.

As you read, consider the following questions:

1. According to Ambrose, what horse had to be euthanized on the track at the 2008 Kentucky Derby because of an injury?

2. How many horses are killed out of every one thousand horses that start a race, as stated by Ambrose?

3. What does the author cite both as a priority and as something that can seem quite difficult?

A horse [Eight Belles] was injured and immediately euthanized in this year's [2008's] running of the Kentucky Derby, and the cry went out that horse racing is cruel and should be outlawed, scuttled, sent to the barn.

No it shouldn't. Reformed? Yes, in some ways. But outlawed? Why? Because of the report that something like 1.6 horses is killed out of every 1,000 horses that start a race?

That's not news you want to cheer about, but is hardly evidence of vast disregard for animals worth huge amounts of money.

Most owners would hardly embrace a system that would too easily make their investments worthless, even if these people were all coldhearted, money-grubbing villains.

Defending the Sport

What the severest critics do not seem to get is that creatures die, all of them, including horses that are not bred for horse racing. And my guess is that few horses receive better overall care than thoroughbred racehorses, whose every muscle twitch is finely analyzed from the day of birth until racing and breeding days are done.

To suppose them unhappy because they are trained and ridden and made to go fast on crowded racetracks is absurd. Read a book like *Seabiscuit*, or listen to horse lovers who have been in the racing business all their lives and you know that the horses often love to run, that some love the attention and some seem to take pride in racing and, not only that, but in winning.

They are born for this thing, you find caring trainers saying, and the worst cruelty just might be to get in the way, especially since they would still be in danger. As one horse breeder has observed in a newspaper piece, accidents also occur when these spirited creatures are racing each other in pastures.

But as expensively coddled as the horses often are—the same breeder mentions a $30,000 operation for one—the case for making some changes in the sport does seem compelling.

Time for Reform

It is emotionally wrenching to learn amidst the excitement of the Derby that a magnificent, beautiful horse like Eight Belles broke her ankles and was swiftly put out of her misery, and so you listen when some say racing can be made safer.

The change some insist should be a priority seems to a layman the most difficult, namely breeding the horses as much for stability as speed. A strong horse that's unlikely to be much of a competitor is going to entice few buyers, and it will obviously require something more than a snap of the fingers to breed animals that are less prone to serious injury but also a genuine threat on the track.

Less challenging would be to make any changes in those tracks that are consistent with what the best science says is least hazardous, or to keep horses from racing too much too young, when their bodies are least able to deal with the physical stress.

The Public May Determine Acceptable Risks

Commentators warn that if some such adjustments do not decrease the fatalities in racing, a sport that has already been fading in public enthusiasm could find itself in dire jeopardy even without laws bringing it to an end, and I suspect that's true.

What also strikes me as true is that there are always those who want to dictate to the rest of us what we can and cannot do, who will opt for the most extreme measure at virtually any provocation and who do not get it that practically all physical activities, both human and animal, entail some degree of risk. Let such people have their way too often, and the world will shrink to the meager limits of their understanding.

> *"So before you permanently mark down a sport as being cruel, think of all the good things it has to offer and how it is learning from its tragedies and mistakes."*

Horse Racing Should Not Be Banned

Chris Antley

Chris Antley is an equestrian and aspiring jockey. In the following viewpoint, she contends that horse racing is not a cruel sport, yet there are cruel practices within the sport that need to be eliminated. Antley acknowledges that many people believe the sport is inhumane; however, these people don't have the right to force their opinion on others.

As you read, consider the following questions:

1. Who is the number one all-time North American money earner, according to Antley?

2. What happened to the European horse George Washington at the Breeders' Cup Classic in 2007?

3. What kind of research did Eight Belles' tragic death inspire, according to the author?

I have been a horse fanatic for almost 6 years now. I am very blessed to witness horse racing's historical moments.

In 2007, I watched Rags to Riches beat the champion male Curlin in the Belmont Stakes. I also watched Curlin win the 2007 Breeders' Cup Classic. In 2008, I saw Big Brown win the Kentucky Derby and Preakness Stakes. I also saw the undefeated Zenyatta win the Ladies' Classic. And also, Curlin winning the Jockey Club Gold Cup becoming the #1 all-time North American money earner, being the only horse to win over 10 million in earnings. In 2009, I saw the long shot Mine That Bird win the Kentucky Derby, the filly Rachel Alexandra win the Haskell and Preakness Stakes, and Summer Bird win the Belmont Stakes and the Travers Stakes. And I saw Zenyatta win the Breeders' Cup Classic.

Also in 2009 I was able to go to a racetrack for my very first time. As a 16th birthday present I went to the Saratoga racetrack. I got to see Kent Desormeaux, Calvin Borel, Johnny Velasquez, Edgar Prado, and more. I also got to meet Mine That Bird's trainer. I was able to get a picture with him and his autograph.

From Triumph to Tragedy

From 2007 to 2009, I have not only been able to witness historical moments, but sadly I have seen racing's tragedies. In 2007, I saw the European horse George Washington break down in the Breeders' Cup Classic. In that year also, I followed the news with Barbaro after he broke down in the Preakness Stakes. In 2008, I watched the filly Eight Belles be put down after breaking down in the Kentucky Derby. And in the Belmont, I watched in horror and shock as I saw Big Brown be pulled up on the top of stretch. And still to this day I can hear the words of the track announcer as he called in disbelief, "And Big Brown has been eased at the top of the stretch." Again, in 2009, I witnessed tragedy. I saw Wanderin Boy being pulled up in the Cigar Mile and later put down.

Top Fifteen Horses by Earnings Since 1976

Rank	Horse Name	Starts	1st	2nd	3rd	Earnings	Win%	Top3	Top3%
1	Curlin	16	11	2	2	$10,501,800	69%	15	94%
2	Cigar	33	19	4	5	$9,999,815	58%	28	85%
3	Skip Away	38	18	10	6	$9,616,360	47%	34	89%
4	Gloria de Campeao	25	9	6	3	$9,258,355	36%	18	72%
5	Fantastic Light	25	12	5	3	$8,486,957	48%	20	80%
6	Invasor	12	11	0	0	$7,804,070	92%	11	92%
7	Pleasantly Perfect	18	9	3	2	$7,789,880	50%	14	78%
8	Smarty Jones	9	8	1	0	$7,613,155	89%	9	100%
9	Zenyatta	20	19	1	0	$7,304,580	95%	20	100%
10	Silver Charm	24	12	7	2	$6,944,369	50%	21	88%
11	Captain Steve	25	9	3	7	$6,828,356	36%	19	76%
12	Alysheba	26	11	8	2	$6,679,242	42%	21	81%
13	Dylan Thomas	20	10	4	1	$6,620,852	50%	15	75%
14	John Henry	83	39	15	9	$6,591,860	47%	63	76%
15	Tiznow	15	8	4	2	$6,427,830	53%	14	93%

TAKEN FROM: Equibase, 2010.

I am not here to brag about myself, but to tell you that all sports have their tragedies. Ever since I became involved in the Sport of Kings, I have heard people say that, "Horse racing is a cruel sport," or "They shouldn't be racing horses so young."

Horse Racing Is Not Cruel

In my opinion, it's not the sport that is cruel, it is the people within the sport that make it that way. Not everyone in horse racing is cruel and yes some things should be changed. Horse racing is learning from its mistakes. Because of the tragedies over the years, it has looked into more ways of making it safer for both horse and rider. For example: poly tracks and the ban of steroids.

Like I said before, every sport has its tragedies and every sport can be cruel. Some of you may think the using of spurs or a whip/crop to be cruel. Those tools/aids weren't made to be cruel. They were made to help reinforce your natural aids. Unfortunately, in the wrong hands, like someone who doesn't know how to use them properly, they can be cruel.

For example, a car may appear to be harmless, but once someone who has been drinking or if someone falls asleep behind the wheel, it can become dangerous.

What I am trying to say is that the sport itself isn't cruel, it's people within it; or a book, fork, butter knife, bottle, etc. can become dangerous depending on who is holding/using it.

Learning from Their Mistakes

Some of you may still think that horse racing is cruel. That is fine, it's your opinion. I am not writing this to change your mind about it, but to open your mind to the fact that "everything" can be cruel and dangerous.

To tell you the truth, I believe that cross-country, harness racing, bull riding and steeplechasing are cruel and dangerous. However, I am not going to force my opinion on you and say that you are a bad person because you like or do that sport.

The tragedies of horse racing are very sad and tragic. Nothing can take away the horror of seeing a horse break down or get injured, but it happens . . . it's life. Yes, it probably could have been prevented, but people have to learn from their mistakes. In my opinion, if it wasn't for Eight Belles, people wouldn't be looking into different kinds of surfaces for the tracks and banning steroids. If it wasn't for Barbaro, we wouldn't be finding a cure for laminitis [an inflammation in the hoof of a horse].

So before you permanently mark down a sport as being cruel, think of all the good things it has to offer and how it is learning from its tragedies and mistakes.

So now it is up to you to determine if a sport is cruel or not.

Periodical and Internet Sources Bibliography

The following articles have been selected to supplement the diverse views presented in this chapter.

Jay Ambrose	"Horse Racing Is in Need of Some Reform, Not Abolition," *Times Herald-Record* (Middletown, NY), May 10, 2008.
Radley Balko	"Gambling (Part 1)," *The Economist*, July 20, 2010.
Leslie Bernal	"Loser-Friendly Casinos," *Boston Globe*, April 12, 2010.
Frank Deford	"Gambling in Delaware Is a Sure Bet," *Sports Illustrated*, May 27, 2009.
Bill Finley	"Industry Can Learn from Greyhound Ban," ESPN.com, December 28, 2009. www.espn.com.
Pat Forde	"Veterinarian: Horse Racing Will Ban Steroid Use," ESPN.com, June 6, 2008. www.espn.com.
Eli Lehrer	"The Risks of Gambling Regulation," *American Spectator*, July 14, 2008.
Michael Mayo	"Should Horse Racing Be Banned? PETA Pounces on Kentucky Derby Tragedy," SunSentinel.com, May 5, 2008. http://weblogs.sun-sentinel.com.
Michelle Rivera	"Is the Future of Florida Greyhound Racing on the Decline?" Examiner.com, April 27, 2010. www.examiner.com.
Kurt Streeter	"States Should Get a Cut of the Sports Betting Action," *Los Angeles Times*, August 30, 2009.

CHAPTER 2

What Are the Economic and Social Implications of Gambling?

Chapter Preface

On May 6, 2006, a four-year-old colt named Barbaro won the world-famous Kentucky Derby. Hopes ran high that the majestic thoroughbred would win the Preakness Stakes—one of the biggest events in American thoroughbred racing—two weeks later and then the Belmont Stakes, becoming the first Triple Crown winner since 1978. During the Preakness, however, Barbaro fractured several bones in and around the ankle of his right hind leg. The next day, he underwent surgery, and veterinarians and other experts expressed hope that after a long rehabilitation, he would be able to walk again. Tragically, Barbaro developed laminitis, a very dangerous disease for horses, in both front legs. Barbaro was euthanized on January 29, 2007.

Two years after Barbaro's injury, another high-profile tragedy in horse racing occurred. During the running of the 2008 Kentucky Derby, a fleet filly named Eight Belles suffered compound fractures of both front ankles after coming in second to the winner, Big Brown. The injury was so catastrophic that the filly had to be euthanized right on the track, with millions of people watching the race and concerned about the horse's fate. It was shocking and upsetting to many that a horse could run a race so magnificently and then be dead in a matter of minutes.

The catastrophic deaths of two such high-profile horses in races broadcast all over the world functioned to turn on a spotlight on the sport of thoroughbred racing. Sportswriters and critics began to investigate the sport, and they didn't like what they saw. It is undeniable that horse racing is a dangerous sport for horses. According to estimates, there are 1.5 career-ending breakdowns for every one thousand racing starts in the United States—an average of two per day.

Sally Jenkins, a sportswriter for the *Washington Post*, stated in an article on May 4, 2008, that "thoroughbred racing is in a moral crisis, and everyone now knows it. Twice since 2006, magnificent animals have suffered catastrophic injuries on live television in Triple Crown races, and there is no explaining that away. Horses are being over-bred and over-raced, until their bodies cannot support their own ambitions, or those of the humans who race them. Barbaro and Eight Belles merely are the most famous horses who have fatally injured themselves."

Supporters of thoroughbred horse racing argue that breakdowns are part of the sport, which does its best to create conditions to protect the stately animals. They maintain that owners love their horses, as do trainers and other staff, and have no interest in putting their investments in danger. Moreover, they point out that thoroughbred horses are like elite athletes who were born to run. They note that horse racing is a sport that has been around for thousands of years; it can be traced back to the nomadic tribesmen of central Asia in 4500 B.C.

The debate over whether horse racing is too dangerous is one of the topics covered in the following chapter, which investigates the economic and social implications of gambling. Other issues under examination are the fiscal impact and social costs of gambling and the benefits of casinos and racinos, which are gambling facilities located inside racetrack establishments.

| "Rather than spending precious time and resources avoiding the law (or, same thing, paying the law off), producers and consumers could more easily get on with business and the huge benefits of working and playing in plain sight."

Gambling Can Generate Much-Needed Revenue

Nick Gillespie

Nick Gillespie is editor in chief of Reason.tv and Reason.com. In the following viewpoint, he proposes the legalization of drugs, prostitution, and gambling. Gillespie argues that by legalizing these vices, the government could tax them, eliminate the black markets for such practices, and raise much-needed revenue from them. He also notes that prohibition rarely works and instead leads to violence and destructive behavior.

As you read, consider the following questions:

1. According to a recent Zogby poll, what percentage of voters support legalizing, taxing, and regulating the growth and sale of marijuana?

Nick Gillespie, "Paying with Our Sins," Reason.com, May 20, 2009. Copyright © 2009 by Reason.com. Reproduced by permission.

2. How much money could legalizing prostitution in Las Vegas annually add to Nevada coffers?

3. According to a 2008 PricewaterhouseCoopers study, how much would legalizing online betting provide in new tax revenue?

The [Barack] Obama administration's drug czar made news recently by saying he wanted to end all loose talk about a "war on drugs." "We're not at war with people in this country," said the czar, Gil Kerlikowske, who favors forcing people into treatment programs rather than jail cells.

Here's a better idea—and one that will help the federal and state governments fill their coffers: Legalize drugs and then tax sales of them. And while we're at it, welcome all forms of gambling (rather than just the few currently and arbitrarily allowed) and let prostitution go legit too. All of these vices, involving billions of dollars and consenting adults, already take place. They just take place beyond the taxman's reach.

Legalizing the world's oldest profession probably wasn't what Rahm Emanuel, the White House chief of staff, meant when he said that we should never allow a crisis to go to waste. But turning America into a Sin City on a Hill could help President Obama pay for his ambitious plans to overhaul health care, invest in green energy, and create gee-whiz trains that whisk "through towns at speeds over 100 miles an hour." More taxed vices would certainly lead to significant new revenue streams at every level. That's one of the reasons 52 percent of voters in a recent Zogby poll said they support legalizing, taxing and regulating the growth and sale of marijuana. Similar cases could be made for prostitution and all forms of gambling.

Economic Benefits of Legalization

In terms of economic stimulation and growth, legalization would end black markets that generate huge amounts of what economists call "deadweight losses," or activity that doesn't contribute to increased productivity. Rather than spending precious time and resources avoiding the law (or, same thing, paying the law off), producers and consumers could more easily get on with business and the huge benefits of working and playing in plain sight.

Consider prostitution. No reliable estimates exist on the number of prostitutes in the United States or aggregate demand for their services. However, Nevada, one of the two states that currently allows paid sex acts, is considering a tax of $5 for each transaction. State Senator Bob Coffin argues further that imposing state taxes on existing brothels could raise $2 million a year (at present, brothels are allowed only in rural counties, which get all the tax revenue), and legalizing prostitution in cities like Las Vegas could swell state coffers by $200 million annually.

A conservative extrapolation from Nevada to the rest of the country would easily mean billions of dollars annually in new tax revenues. Rhode Island, which has never explicitly banned prostitution, is on the verge of finally doing so—but with the state facing a $661 million budget shortfall, perhaps fully legalizing the vice (and then taking a cut) would be the smarter play.

Every state except Hawaii and Utah already permits various types of gambling, from state lotteries to racetracks to casinos. In 2007, such activity generated more than $92 billion in receipts, much of which was earmarked for the elderly and education. Representative Barney Frank, Democrat of Massachusetts, has introduced legislation to repeal the federal ban on online gambling; and a 2008 study by Pricewaterhouse-Coopers estimates that legalizing cyberspace betting alone could yield as much as $5 billion a year in new tax revenues. Add to that expanded opportunities for less exotic forms of wagering at, say, the local watering hole and the tax figure would be vastly larger.

Based on estimates from the White House Office of National Drug Control Policy, Americans spend at least $64 billion a year on illegal drugs. And according to a 2006 study by the former president of the National Organization for the Reform of Marijuana Laws, Jon Gettman, marijuana is already the top cash crop in a dozen states and among the top five crops in 39 states, with a total annual value of $36 billion.

A 2005 cost-benefit analysis of marijuana prohibition by Jeffrey Miron, a Harvard economist, calculated that ending marijuana prohibition would save $7.7 billion in direct state and federal law enforcement costs while generating more than $6 billion a year if it were taxed at the same rate as alcohol and tobacco. The drug czar's office says that a gram of pure cocaine costs between $100 and $150; a gram of heroin almost $400; and a bulk gram of marijuana between $15 and $20. Those transactions are now occurring off the books of business and government alike.

History Shows Prohibition Does Not Work

As the history of alcohol prohibition underscores, there are also many noneconomic reasons to favor legalization of vices: Prohibition rarely achieves its desired goals and instead increases violence (when was the last time a tobacco kingpin was killed in a deal gone wrong?) and destructive behavior (it's hard enough to get help if you're a substance abuser and that much harder if you're a criminal too). And by policing vice, law enforcement is too often distracted at best or corrupted at worst, as familiar headlines about cops pocketing bribes and seized drugs attest. There's a lot to be said for treating consenting adults like, well, adults.

But there is an economic argument as well, one that Franklin Roosevelt understood when he promised to end Prohibition during the 1932 presidential campaign. "Our tax burden would not be so heavy nor the forms that it takes so objectionable," thundered Roosevelt, "if some reasonable propor-

Gaming Revenue: Ten-Year Trends

Year	Total Commercial Casino	Total Gaming
2000	24.50*	$61.4
2001	$25.70*	$63.3
2002	$26.50*	$68.6
2003	$27.02*	$72.9
2004	$28.93	$78.8
2005	$30.37	$84.4
2006	$32.42	$90.9
2007	$34.13	$92.3
2008	$32.54	N/A
2009	$30.74	N/A

Note: All amounts in billions.
*Amount does not include deepwater cruise ships, cruises-to-nowhere or non-casino devices.

TAKEN FROM: American Gaming Association, Christiansen Capital Advisors LLC.

tion of the unaccountable millions now paid to those whose business had been reared upon this stupendous blunder could be made available for the expense of government."

Roosevelt could also have talked about how legitimate fortunes can be made out of goods and services associated with vice. Part of his family fortune came from the opium trade, after all, and he and other leaders during the Depression oversaw a generally orderly, re-legalization of the nation's breweries and distilleries.

There's every reason to believe that today's drug lords could go legit as quickly, and easily as, say, Ernest and Julio Gallo, the venerable winemakers who once sold their product to Al Capone [an organized crime figure]. Indeed, here's a (I hope soon-to-be-legal) bet worth making: If marijuana is legalized, look for the scion of a marijuana plantation operation to be president within 50 years.

Legalizing vice will not balance government deficits by itself—that will largely depend on spending cuts, which seem beyond the reach of all politicians. But in a time when every penny counts and the economy needs stimulation, allowing prostitution, gambling and drugs could give us all a real lift.

> *"[Gambling] siphons money out of the private economy just as tax increases do and hardly ever accomplishes what government advocates promise it will."*

Relying on Gambling Revenue Is Poor Fiscal Policy

Steven Malanga

Steven Malanga is a contributing editor to City Journal, *a columnist for RealClearMarkets.com, and a senior fellow at the Manhattan Institute for Policy Research. In the following viewpoint, he contends that the recent trend of states legalizing gambling to close budget gaps is bad fiscal policy. Malanga argues that state-sponsored gambling may be even more harmful to private economies than a typical tax increase because the government's take is so high. He also notes gambling takes a disproportionate toll on the poor.*

As you read, consider the following questions:

1. According to Malanga, how many US states have legalized some form of gambling?

Steven Malanga, "States Place Bad Bets with Gambling," Manhattan Institute for Policy Research, June 24, 2009. Copyright © 2009, Manhattan Institute for Policy Research. Reproduced by permission of Realclearmarkets.com.

2. How many states passed or considered passing new gambling initiatives in 2009, according to the viewpoint?

3. What percentage of gross income do households earning under $12,500 spend on the lottery on average, as cited by the author?

In *Guys and Dolls*, craps players desperate for diversion welcome the arrival of Nathan Detroit because "even when the heat is on it's never too hot" for Nathan to arrange some action.

Today, Nathan Detroit is more likely to be a state legislator, a governor or a board of education commissioner than a Broadway gambler. Forty-eight of our states have now legalized at least some form of gambling, and in the wake of growing state budget woes, legislators are scrambling to expand government-controlled legalized betting to raise new revenues. Every recession, in fact, brings a little more state-authorized betting, so that what started out as a few state lotteries has grown to government-chartered casinos, sports wagering, slots machines at racetracks, and keno parlors—to name just a few areas of public-sector sanctioned betting. This year [2009] at least a dozen states have passed or are considering new gambling initiatives, after half a dozen new ones last year [2008].

A Disturbing Trend

You don't have to be a moralist to recoil at this trend because expanding legalized gambling to close budget gaps is lousy fiscal policy. It siphons money out of the private economy just as tax increases do and hardly ever accomplishes what government advocates promise it will. Typical is the phony relationship between education financing and lotteries, which are often promoted to taxpayers as a painless way to boost public school spending or support other programs. "Sold to the electorate on the grounds that they will reduce taxes or provide better services, lotteries do neither," concluded Thomas H.

An Attack on State and Local Governments

I'm completely in favor of allowing citizens to do anything they want with their money. It's theoretically a free country and if people chose to gamble with their disposable income rather than contribute to their 401(k) or kids' college fund, that is their choice. What I do object to is state and local governments turning to gambling in an attempt to plug their budget deficits caused by doling out ungodly generous benefits to state union workers and frivolous wasteful pork projects designed to get lawmakers re-elected. The facts are that gambling negatively impacts the uneducated poor, senior citizens, and young adults the most.

James Quinn,
"Americans Gambling $100 Billion in
Casinos Like Rats in a Cage," Casino Watch,
October 11, 2009. http://casinowatch.org.

Jones, co-author of *America's Gamble,* after a series of studies in the early 1990s. "They become one of government's false promises." Indeed, Jones and others have found that states with lotteries dedicated to education spend no more money proportionally on public schools than other states. Nor are taxes on average lower in such states.

There's evidence that state lotteries work on a private economy in the same way that tax increases do—by taking money that would be spent on goods and services and giving it to government. Of course, you'll never hear this from advocates of state-sponsored gambling, who typically argue that it merely captures money that people are already betting illegally anyway. Under this rationale, expanding government gambling sends money into public coffers painlessly.

But a 2002 National Bureau of Economic Research study authored by economist Melissa Schettini Kearney looked at consumer expenditures in 21 states that instituted a lottery between 1982 and 1998 and concluded that household spending declined by an average of $137 per quarter in each state in the first year of the lottery. That decline corresponded closely to average expenditures per adult on the lottery, suggesting to Kearney that "spending on lottery tickets is financed completely by a reduction in non-gambling expenditures." How is this possible? Because gamblers don't reduce their illegal betting when the state introduces a new game; they gamble more, surveys show. That's why new state gambling initiatives reallocate money already in the economy, passing more of it through public coffers.

True Economic Effects of State-Sponsored Gambling

In fact, state-sponsored gambling may have a more harmful impact on a private economy than your typical tax increase, because government's take is so high. The Tax Foundation, for instance, estimates that the implicit average tax rate of state lotteries is a whopping 43 percent because states pay out only half of the betting proceeds and spend about 7 percent of revenues to administer the lottery. Of course, few bettors understand that's the payout/tax rate, which is one reason why the Tax Foundation argues that lotteries are bad fiscal policy— because they are taxes that lack transparency.

Lottery advocates say that the high tax rate is irrelevant since gambling is a discretionary activity, something that you can simply forgo. But government justifies high tax rates on other products—cigarettes, alcohol, gasoline—on the grounds that society wants people to use less of them. By contrast, states spend millions of dollars trying to persuade us to gamble more. As the historian and social critic Barbara Dafoe White-head, who calls lotteries 'anti-thrift' institutions, has observed, governments "don't simply make [lotteries] available: They actively seek to 'grow' their market . . . work hard to hold onto current players, entice new players into the game and increase the frequency of play."

And the effort succeeds disproportionately among the poor, something we've known for years. Back in the mid-1980s, for instance, one study estimated that adults making under $10,000 spent three times more per week on state lotteries than those earning $50,000 or more annually. Moreover, the study found that the burden was concentrated in 20 percent of households that gambled the most. Among those earning under $10,000 annually, the most frequent gamblers spent $35.66 a week, or $1,855 a year. Today, the pattern persists. Households earning under $12,500 a year spend five percent of gross income on the lottery, compared to one-third of one percent in households earning ten times as much.

Looking for a Lucky Score

Today states market lotteries with slogans like "A Ticket and a Dream," or "Just Imagine." That makes it a great irony that some states pitch the lottery as a revenue raiser for education, because once upon a time our public schools taught that the American dream was to achieve success through the Protestant ethic—hard work, thrift and a patient accumulation of wealth, not the big, improbable, lucky score.

While recessions have typically brought incremental increases in government involvement in gambling, we're looking at major shifts now, especially in states that run big budget deficits where politicians can rarely make the tough fiscal choices. New Jersey legislators (fiscally irresponsible case #1) are now contemplating suing the federal government to allow Jersey into sports betting, which would presumably prompt a rush into this fertile new field. (Only four states can permit sports betting without federal approval because they had laws on the books back when Congress banned the practice for everyone else).

There's an old saying in betting that if you're in a poker game and you look around the table and can't tell who the sucker is, it's probably you. That's something that taxpayers have yet to realize when it comes to government gambling schemes.

| "[For] a few unfortunate young people and their families, the Road to the Final Four, the nation's fourth biggest gambling event, is paved with personal and financial ruin." |

Gambling Is Harmful and Causes Human Suffering

Michael McCarthy

Michael McCarthy is a reporter for USA Today. *In the following viewpoint, he warns young people filling out their National Collegiate Athletic Association (NCAA) "March Madness" brackets that gambling is a harmful vice that can lead to personal and financial ruin. McCarthy describes several incidents of young people who have gotten involved with gambling and the horrific toll it took on their lives.*

As you read, consider the following questions:

1. According to a 2004 study by the NCAA, did the league find evidence of sports wagering?

2. How much is illegally wagered on the NCAA "March Madness" tournament every year?

Michael McCarthy, "Gambling Madness Can Snag Court Fans," *USA Today*, March 28, 2007. Copyright © 2007 USA TODAY, a division of Gannett Co. Inc. Reproduced by permission.

3. According to McCarthy, what was the percentage of males seventeen and older who said they gamble over the Internet on a weekly basis in 2006?

Most of the people giddily filling out brackets for their NCAA [National Collegiate Athletic Association] "March Madness" office pool will never have a problem. But for a few unfortunate young people and their families, the Road to the Final Four, the nation's fourth biggest gambling event, is paved with personal and financial ruin.

Some college students addicted to sports betting or online poker have taken it to extremes. They have committed crimes, including bank robbery and murder, over gambling debts. Others, unable to face the guilt or consequences of betting away tuition, have committed suicide.

The NCAA hopes the student-athletes in the men's and women's basketball tournaments won't be among them. To that end it is launching a national study this year [2007] to try to measure how many student-athletes across sports are betting on games, taking money to throw games or sharing inside information. Results will be released in 2008. The last study, released in 2004, found "disturbing" evidence of sports wagering.

The FBI, meanwhile, is on the lookout for tampering with student-athletes in Atlanta, site of the men's Final Four. During last year's round of 16, a player got a suspicious text-mail asking for inside information, says Rachel Newman Baker, NCAA director of agents, gambling and amateurism activity. She won't name him.

The Human Toll

If the NCAA wants information on the human toll from gambling, it should ask Sandi Snook. The 41-year-old mother from Charles City, Iowa, says she lost two 17-year-old sons, directly or indirectly, to the sports betting addiction of Meng-Ju "Mark" Wu, a 19-year-old freshman at the University of Wisconsin.

Dane County (Wis.) prosecutors said Wu, furious over a $15,000 sports betting debt, shot Snook's son Dustin Wilson to death in his sleep June 26, 2003, in Verona, Wis., with Wu's bookie Jason McGuigan, 28, and Dan Swanson, 25. McGuigan was the real target, says Bernie Coughlin, Verona's police chief. Wilson and Swanson, McGuigan's roommates, were in the wrong place at the wrong time. Hours before his trial was to begin, Wu hung himself in jail Jan. 17, 2005.

Wilson's death devastated his brother and best friend, David, and Nov. 19, 2005, David Snook locked the door of his bedroom and hung himself in his closet.

"My advice to kids about gambling is don't do it, don't think about it, don't even be around anybody who does it," Sandi Snook says.

Wu committed the triple-homicide, Coughlin says, shortly after his parents confronted him about gambling away his tuition and expense money with an online sports book.

"It was too much for him, the embarrassment, the shame of losing the money," Coughlin says.

Lure of NCAA Betting Great

Money drives the real March Madness. The $6 billion illegally wagered on the NCAA tournament through office pools, on-line sports books and street corner bookies trails the $8.5 billion bet on the Super Bowl, *USA Today* sports analyst Danny Sheridan says. Final Four games will generate $2.25 billion in illegal betting, he predicts.

"It's like spring break for sports bettors," Sheridan says.

Bracketology fever reaches its apex in Las Vegas. The money legally wagered on college and professional basketball last March more than doubled to $195.7 million from $95.9 million in February, says Frank Streshley, senior analyst for

Nevada Gaming Control Board. The total then fell by more than two-thirds to $59.2 million in April.

Organized crime members target student-athletes because they're easy marks, says Michael Franzese, a former mobster with the Colombo Mafia family in Brooklyn.

Many think they know college sports better than pro sports. Once they lose, they commit the typical mistake of "squares," or amateur gamblers, trying to play their way back to even—and end up deeper in the hole.

At that point, they're faced with the choice of paying money they don't have or doing something they don't want to do.

"If they lose money, and most do, what other options do they have?" Franzese asks. "They don't have much money. A lot of them don't have jobs because they're so wrapped up with sports and their school. They don't want to go to their parents and admit their problem. So they end up stealing, or do something worse, to make up money they owe.

"They're surprisingly naive and unsophisticated," says Franzese, who has spoken about the perils of betting at more than 175 Division I college campuses.

One-third of the callers to the toll-free help line 1-888-LastBet (1-888-527-8238) are 12–25, says Arnie Wexler, a recovering compulsive gambler.

The percentage of males 17 and older who say they gamble over the Internet on a weekly basis jumped to 5.8% in 2006, a 100% increase from the previous year, according to the National Annenberg Survey of Youth.

Lifestyle Can Turn Dangerous

The son of a wealthy Taiwanese family, Wu enrolled at Wisconsin to study Chinese in 2002. He befriended McGuigan, a known gambler/bookie, to gain access to his world. McGuigan set up an offshore gambling account for Wu and charged him for betting tips about American sports.

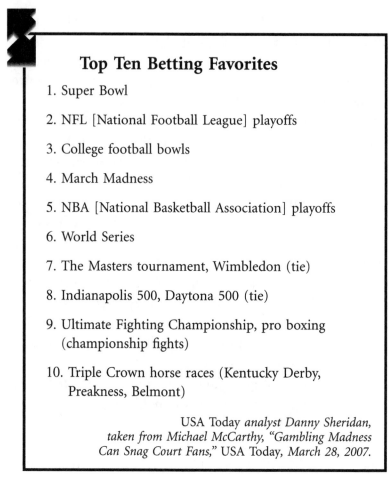

Top Ten Betting Favorites

1. Super Bowl

2. NFL [National Football League] playoffs

3. College football bowls

4. March Madness

5. NBA [National Basketball Association] playoffs

6. World Series

7. The Masters tournament, Wimbledon (tie)

8. Indianapolis 500, Daytona 500 (tie)

9. Ultimate Fighting Championship, pro boxing (championship fights)

10. Triple Crown horse races (Kentucky Derby, Preakness, Belmont)

USA Today *analyst Danny Sheridan,*
taken from Michael McCarthy, "Gambling Madness
Can Snag Court Fans," USA Today, *March 28, 2007.*

The relationship apparently turned murderous, Coughlin says, when Wu discovered McGuigan was lying to him: that Wu had lost, not won, thousands betting on sports.

The New York Police Department arrested Wu as he was about to return to Taiwan.

In custody, Wu admitted his gambling addiction to police. McGuigan father's, Robert, told WISC-TV's News 3 in Madison that his son owed $20,000 or more to bookies in Illinois.

"I've got triple guilt, for my son and for the others," he told the *Capital Times* of Madison.

Both Wu and McGuigan were seduced by the idea of money for nothing, Coughlin says, that they could make big bucks and drive expensive cars without working for it: "They got wrapped up into a lifestyle that was a fraud, a dangerous lifestyle that obviously reached the point of no return."

Suicides Not Uncommon

Cleveland police concluded Joseph Kupchik, 19, stabbed himself in the chest with a knife and then jumped from the ninth floor of a Cleveland parking garage Feb. 12, 2006, Lt. Thomas Stacho says. The accounting student at Cleveland's Cuyahoga Community College lost a considerable amount of money in online gambling in the weeks before his death, Stacho says.

Kupchik bet $500 on Georgetown to win the 2006 NCAA men's basketball championship, eventually won by Florida, the (Cleveland) *Plain Dealer* reported. He also transferred more than $3,500 in tuition money to his checking account, the paper reported, while paying more than $3,400 to a gambling website in the Caribbean.

Policeman's Family Rocked

On the eve of last year's NCAA basketball tournament, the son of a Midwest police chief was arrested on charges of operating an illegal bookmaking operation catering to Catholic high school students in the Chicago area.

Daniel Dalzell, 23-year-old son of then-Alsip (Ill.) police chief Rick Dalzell, pleaded guilty to misdemeanor gambling charges Nov. 22 and was sentenced to two years' probation and $5,000 in court costs and fines, says Tandra Simonton, spokeswoman for the Cook County (Ill.) State's Attorney's Office.

From Nov. 1, 2005, to March 8, 2006, Dalzell, who had no criminal record, booked bets on college and pro games for 10–12 students at his alma mater, Marist High School, as well as St. Rita's high school, Simonton says. Some kids ran up tabs as high as $27,000.

When they were allegedly threatened with collection, they panicked and ran to the cops.

'Perfect Student' Caught Up

The class president-turned-bank robber story of Gregory Hogan Jr. proved to be an irresistible cautionary tale for the media, *The New York Times Magazine* noted last year.

The former sophomore class president at Lehigh University in Bethlehem, Pa., appeared to be the perfect student. The home-schooled son of a Baptist preacher, Hogan Jr. was a piano prodigy who played Carnegie Hall twice before 14. But he became hooked on online poker at Lehigh.

When his father, the Rev. Gregory Hogan Sr., placed anti-gambling software blocks on his computer, his son played Texas Hold 'Em for up to 10 hours at a time in the school library.

Drinking heavily, he became despondent about his debts to fraternity brothers, his father says. He stole $2,000 in bonds from the family to finance his addiction.

Then the unarmed Hogan Jr. stood in line before handing over a note claiming he had a gun and demanding money from a teller at an Allentown, Pa., bank Dec. 9, 2005. He made no attempt to conceal his identity and left with $2,871.

He went to the movies to see *The Chronicles of Narnia* with a couple of unsuspecting friends and then treated his fraternity pals to pizza. Cops arrested him within hours when he showed up, cello in hand, for orchestra practice on campus. He confessed immediately.

Now 21, he's serving time at a state prison in Pennsylvania.

"Greg stood in line because he's a polite young man," his father says. "This was the compulsion, the black hole of gambling he was caught up in. He felt this was the only thing he could do."

> *"A free society where the government bans activities it finds immoral or unseemly is not really a free society."*

Gambling Bans Encroach on Civil Liberties

Radley Balko

Radley Balko is a senior editor at Reason *magazine. In the following viewpoint, he contends that prohibition of consensual crimes like gambling cannot be enforced without encroaching on the privacy and civil liberties of citizens involved in the practice. Balko argues that any society that bans activities it finds immoral or unsavory is not truly a free society.*

As you read, consider the following questions:

1. What happened to suspected gambler Sal Culosi in January 2006, according to Balko?

2. What does prohibiting gambling do, according to the author?

3. According to the viewpoint, what happened when the American government attempted to ban online gambling in 2006?

In January 2006, the Fairfax County, Virginia, Police Department sent a SWAT (Special Weapons and Tactics) team to the home of Sal Culosi, a 37-year-old optometrist. Several months earlier, a detective had overheard Mr Culosi and some friends making a wager on a college football game they were watching at a sports bar. The detective joined in the wagering, befriended Mr Culosi, then continued to bet on games with him, suggesting higher and higher wagers until they hit the minimum amount needed to charge Mr Culosi with running a gambling operation. During the raid, one SWAT officer fired his gun, he says by accident. The bullet struck Mr Culosi directly in the heart, killing him.

Months later, as the NCAA (National Collegiate Athletic Association) basketball tournament was about to start, the same police department that had just killed a man for betting on sports put out a press release warning residents not to wager on tournament office pools, ominously titled "Illegal Gambling Not Worth the Risk". That same year, 2006, the Virginia state government spent $20m [million] encouraging its citizens to play the state lottery.

Bans Do Not Work

Gambling is no different from any other consensual crime. Prohibiting it does not make it go away. It merely pushes it underground, where it is impossible to monitor for cheating and fraud, where the stakes are likely to be higher, and where problem gamblers stand to lose quite a bit more than merely their pay packet. When you make a popular activity illegal, you also create new sources of funding for career criminals. It is fairly well known that America's experiment with alcohol prohibition gave rise to the mob. But Al Capone [an organized crime figure] and his rivals also brought in big money from the numbers racket.

Consensual crimes like gambling also produce no aggrieved victim to report or provide evidence of the crime. All parties to a sports wager or illegal card game participate willingly. So in order to enforce these laws, police must go out and search for criminal activity. This creates a number of problems.

Three Problems with Prohibition

First, it distorts policing priorities. If there are no murder victims or reported car thefts, homicide and property crimes, cops are not expected to go out and arrest people anyway. But there will always be gambling. It is just a matter of finding it. A vice cop is always expected to bring in gamblers and bookies. This creates the sort of incentive problems that cause police to send SWAT teams to the homes of people who harmlessly wager on college sports with friends, or to veterans' halls that run charity poker games. Whether explicit or implied, vice police face quotas. It is easier to fill them with harmless gamblers than to conduct months-long investigations into major criminal enterprises. And every cop spent investigating a bookie or neighbourhood poker game is one less cop investigating crimes that produce actual victims.

Second, the government cannot enforce a ban on gambling without intruding on the privacy and civil liberties of its citizens. When the American government attempted to ban online gambling in 2006, the preamble to the bill noted that "traditional law enforcement mechanisms are often inadequate" to enforce these sorts of bans. So the government deputized banks to police their customers' accounts, and to block and report payments to gaming sites. There was even talk of forcing Internet service providers to monitor their customers' web habits. The bill ended up criminalising foreign companies that facilitate online payments because in addition to thousands of other clients, those companies also worked with gaming sites, even though doing so was perfectly legal in the countries where those companies were located. (The American government has actually arrested executives from those companies.) To enforce America's drug prohibition, another ban on consensual crimes, the government has granted itself so many powers to violate its citizens' civil liberties that some legal scholars now refer to a "drug war exception" to the Bill of Rights.

Lastly, enforcement of consensual crimes often requires police to break the very laws they are enforcing (as the detective did in the Culosi case)—or pay an informant to do it for them. This undermines respect for the rule of law, tempts law enforcement into corruption and often produces bad information.

Policing Gambling Is Not the Job of Government

But the strongest argument for legalising gambling is also the simplest: individual liberty. A free society where the government bans activities it finds immoral or unseemly is not really a free society. Proponents of gambling prohibition say gambling is an addiction, and often point to stories of addicts who have wagered away the kids' college fund, lost their house, or turned to crime to pay off their debts. But foolishness with our own money should not be illegal. We do not prohibit people from blowing their savings on eBay, taking out mortgages or loans they cannot afford (at least not yet), or frittering away their pay packets on mistresses. The government has no business policing its citizens' personal lives for bad habits (particularly when it is happy to exploit those same habits for its own benefit). If liberty means anything at all, it means the freedom to make our own choices about our own lives, our money, our habits and how we spend our leisure time, even if they happen to be choices other people would not make for themselves.

> *"Many parts of the gambling industry are struggling during the economic downturn, and no one is sure how long the slump will continue."*

Racinos Hurt the Economy

Adam Ragusea

Adam Ragusea is a reporter for WBUR radio in Boston. In the following viewpoint, he illustrates that although slot machines make money, racinos—racetrack establishments where slot machines are available—tend to attract "convenience gamblers" and therefore would be an overall drag on the state economy. Ragusea reports that racinos must attract money from outside of the local areas—like big casinos do—to really make a long-term difference.

As you read, consider the following questions:

1. What percentage of the casinos in Atlantic City are in bankruptcy, according to Ragusea?

2. As of 2010, how much has revenue at Foxwoods Casino in Connecticut decreased?

Adam Ragusea, "'Racinos' Could Be Good for State Coffers, Bad for Economy," WBUR90.9 FM and wbur.org, March 5, 2010. Copyright © 2010, WBUR.org. Reproduced by permission.

3. According to the viewpoint, how much does a slot machine cost?

Massachusetts House Speaker Robert DeLeo made the case for legalizing gambling in the state on Thursday [in March 2010], saying his proposed measures would generate badly needed revenue and create jobs for blue-collar workers.

But how substantial could those benefits be? Many parts of the gambling industry are struggling during the economic downturn, and no one is sure how long the slump will continue.

Bill Thompson is a professor of public administration at the University of Nevada, Las Vegas, which, as you might imagine, is probably the world center for the academic study of gambling. I asked him the big question: How's the industry doing right now?

"Poor! One word: Poorly!" Thompson told me.

The gaming industry in Thompson's backyard is off 30 percent from its 2008 peak. Outside of Vegas, a quarter of the casinos in Atlantic City are in bankruptcy.

As for our neck of the woods?

The Situation in the Northeast

"Foxwoods isn't doing very well, and Foxwoods is the premier casino in the world, the largest in the world," he said. "Boy, if they're not doing well, something's wrong."

Revenue at the Connecticut giant is down about 20 percent. Last fall, 700 employees got the axe.

But the trend has been different among the smaller slot parlors and "racinos," according to Clyde Barrow.

No, not that Clyde Barrow. I'm talking about the Clyde Barrow from UMass Dartmouth, who has been quoted in every other gambling story since Gov. Deval Patrick got elected.

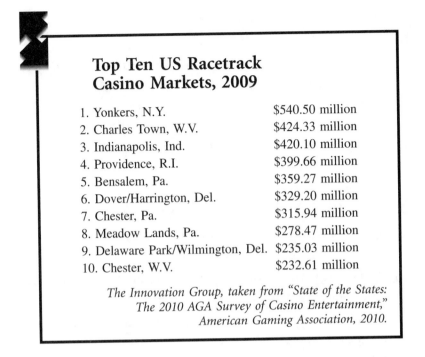

Top Ten US Racetrack Casino Markets, 2009

1. Yonkers, N.Y.	$540.50 million
2. Charles Town, W.V.	$424.33 million
3. Indianapolis, Ind.	$420.10 million
4. Providence, R.I.	$399.66 million
5. Bensalem, Pa.	$359.27 million
6. Dover/Harrington, Del.	$329.20 million
7. Chester, Pa.	$315.94 million
8. Meadow Lands, Pa.	$278.47 million
9. Delaware Park/Wilmington, Del.	$235.03 million
10. Chester, W.V.	$232.61 million

The Innovation Group, taken from "State of the States: The 2010 AGA Survey of Casino Entertainment," American Gaming Association, 2010.

"The 'racinos' have done better across the East Coast than the resort casinos have."

I should note that Barrow has been criticized by some for taking industry money for his research.

"Convenience Gambling"

Barrow said our recession-era tendency to look for kicks closer to home has actually been a boon to so-called "convenience gambling," small parlors like the ones in Maine and Rhode Island.

"Give you an example: Revenues at Twin River, despite their financial problems, have actually continued to go up right through the recession, the same is true of Hollywood slots in Bangor, Maine," Barrow said. (Overbuilding during the boom years has landed Twin River in bankruptcy proceedings, but revenue has been growing dramatically.)

He said that's one reason why Speaker DeLeo is pushing 'racinos'—to rake in instant cash.

"What the racetrack casinos hold out is the opportunity to collect some licensing fees right up front, as well as some actual slot machine tax revenue," Barrow said. "I mean they're already licensed gambling facilities, most of them have empty space, you can put slot machines in there in a comparatively short period of time."

Promises of Reviving a Ghost Town

In Raynham, at the now-defunct dog track, manager Karen Roberts stands in the grandstand area.

"In its day, it was always packed, and you had the full line of tellers," she says, wistfully.

It has been empty since Dec. 31, 2009, when the state ban on greyhound racing took effect.

Today, this hundred-acre facility is a ghost town, a vast expanse of darkened chambers broken up with isolated pockets of light, where handfuls of mostly white-haired gamblers huddle around televisions simulcasting races from hundreds of miles away.

One man, who says he has patronized Raynham for 52 years, hopes for a nursing home in the infield.

Changes to Come?

This eerie quiet could change if DeLeo's proposed legislation passes.

"Between 60 and 90 days, they'd have a thousand slots that they could have up and running," Roberts says.

A thousand?

"Yeah. They're shooting for 2,500 but that would be over a 12-month time," she says. The racetrack would probably become a parking lot.

Roberts says she would be sad to see that happen, but, "you know it's part of the times, you gotta keep up with the times."

And Roberts does perk at the prospect of hiring back some of the 400 or so people she had to lay off last year. But even if those jobs come back, University of Nevada Professor Bill Thompson said slots at the tracks would probably be a net drag on the Massachusetts economy.

"The slot machine costs $15,000 dollars, you're losing that just when you buy the machine, and then if the gamblers are just local money, you never make it up," Thompson said.

Remember, parlors in Maine and Rhode Island owe their relative success right now to the fact that they serve local markets. So, Thompson said, if only Bay Staters go to the "racinos," our overall economy loses money.

"Yet at the same time, because the 'racino' makes money, the state will see more tax revenue. So it can be good for the politicians and the budget makers, but bad for the economy," Thompson said.

On the other hand, Speaker DeLeo says that infusion of revenue could be directed into a special fund to foster much-needed blue-collar jobs beyond the gaming industry.

> *"The appeal of the absolutely random, quick-win-or-lose slots experience is propping up an industry that filled grandstands in the 20th century with savvy, studious racing enthusiasts."*

Racinos Have Economic Benefits

Gary Rotstein

Gary Rotstein is a reporter with the Pittsburgh Post-Gazette. *In the following viewpoint, he documents the trend toward racinos—racetrack establishments equipped with slot machines—in many states. Rotstein finds that racinos have become more popular than traditional racetracks, providing much-need revenue to supplement the struggling sport of horse racing. He also notes that racinos are credited with saving the horse and dog racing industries in several states and have become a priority for investors in the racing industry.*

As you read, consider the following questions:

1. According to Rotstein, how much does Harrah's Chester Casino and Racetrack draw weekly in slots revenue?

2. How much did Prairie Meadows Racetrack and Casino earn in 2006 from slots, according to the viewpoint?

3. How much did the amount wagered on thoroughbred racing increase from 1990 to 2005, as cited by the author?

Ray and Elayne Vasvari never saw a single horse during their six hours at Mountaineer [Casino,] Race Track & Resort on Thursday [in February 2007], one of the three days a week the thoroughbreds don't even run in Chester, W.Va.

But the couple from Struthers, Ohio, 50 miles away, couldn't have cared less. They never play the horses on their twice-weekly visits. They had their fun on the slot machines, lost some money, had a meal and headed home content.

"I've got no faith in the horse racing system," explained Ray Vasvari, 70. "I wouldn't have the patience to figure it out. I don't have the knowledge."

The Vasvaris are representative of America's decades-long shift toward wagers with immediate gratification, a trend that has been accelerated by the "racinos" that are sweeping into Pennsylvania like so many thundering hooves across a finish line.

Racetracks Turn to Slot Machines

Three racetrack casinos in Eastern Pennsylvania that have added slots in recent months all met or surpassed expectations in public interest and wagering on the machines. Western Pennsylvania gets it first taste this week, with Wednesday's 9 A.M. debut of Presque Isle Downs & Casino in Erie County. Another slots parlor is to follow at The Meadows harness track in Washington County in May.

In most or all of these cases, racetrack operators will be getting at least 90 percent of their revenue from slot machines. The appeal of the absolutely random, quick-win-or-lose slots experience is propping up an industry that filled grandstands in the 20th century with savvy, studious racing enthusiasts.

The conversion to racinos is credited with saving the horse and dog racing industries over the past decade in West Virginia, which was among the first states to add casinos to its tracks. Pennsylvania enters the field as a result of a 2004 law that was conceived with help from the racing industry, whose operators long complained they were losing out to the pioneer racino competitors.

Reasons for Racinos

While Pennsylvania is unique in adding five large stand-alone parlors to the slots mix, including the Majestic Star Casino to open on the North Side in 2008, a dozen states have chosen racinos over Vegas-style casinos since the mid-1990s. Several factors help drive the trend:

- The gambling expansion takes place at locations with a history of wagering, minimizing the opposition from local antigambling groups.

- Buildings, parking and other infrastructure are already in place, usually on spacious property, reducing development costs and enabling higher tax rates than is often the case in casino states.

- States can help areas around racinos with jobs and support for agricultural industries. The new gambling revenue will not only flow to state and local governments and track operators, but it will also increase racing purses to boost the livelihoods of horse owners, breeders, jockeys and trainers. In many cases, industry representatives and analysts say, the slots have been the only way to sustain tracks where public interest has sagged since the 1980s.

"You could look at it as rewarding people for keeping racing going, but you can also look at it as rewarding an industry that has essentially failed," said Bennett Liebman, coordinator of the Albany Law School Racing and Gaming Law program. "The fact is these really are casinos or slot parlors with a side interest in racing."

Changing Priorities

Thoroughbred racing won't even begin until around Sept. 1 at Presque Isle Downs, the new facility a few hundred yards off Interstate 90 owned by MTR Gaming Group Inc., which also owns Mountaineer. The company had to set construction priorities, said Presque Isle Chief Executive Officer Richard Knight, and the preparations for 2,000 slot machines came ahead of those for the mile-long oval track. Projections from the racino's consultant are that the slots will bring in more than $140 million annually, once fully operating, and the horses less than $5 million.

Presque Isle is one of the few new racetracks in America in recent years, with another, Harrah's Chester casino and racetrack outside Philadelphia, drawing as much as $6 million weekly in slots revenue since opening in January [2010].

MTR President Edson "Ted" Arneault said he would have developed Presque Isle as a track even without slots approval, but it would have been a much smaller investment—about $18 million instead of $250 million—and it would not have been the "home run" he expects from the racino. He expects success even though it is not the full hotel-and-activities resort that Mountaineer is, and projected revenues are among the smallest of any of the Pennsylvania slots parlors.

West Virginia's legislature approved slots connected to its lottery system in 1994, a decade ahead of Pennsylvania. If that hadn't happened, Mr. Arneault said, Mountaineer today would probably still exist, "but it would have been limping along, much like other tracks that don't have slots."

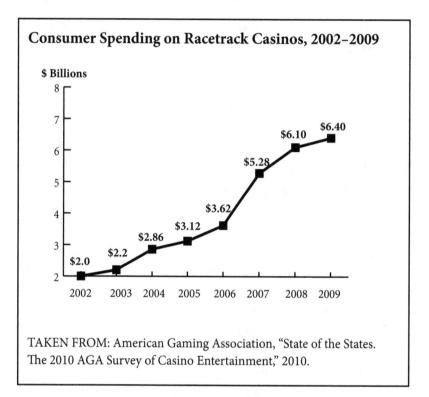

Consumer Spending on Racetrack Casinos, 2002–2009

TAKEN FROM: American Gaming Association, "State of the States. The 2010 AGA Survey of Casino Entertainment," 2010.

More States Considering Racinos

Delaware, Iowa, Louisiana, Maine, New Mexico, New York, Oklahoma and Rhode Island also preceded Pennsylvania in providing slots at racetracks. The machines also arrived at tracks in Florida late last year, just as in Pennsylvania.

West Virginia lawmakers are now debating adding table games at its four horse and dog tracks to offset the competition of Pennsylvania's slots parlors. In almost all other cases, however, operators are content to draw customers with only the slot machines, which have lower overhead costs and draw the majority of people anyway.

Prairie Meadows Racetrack and Casino in Altoona, Iowa, outside Des Moines, began offering table games in 2004 after receiving legislative authorization. Its revenue breakdown in 2006 from its three types of gambling: $163.8 million from slots, $18.8 million from table games, and $4.6 million from pari-mutuel betting, or horse wagering.

In some cases, the addition of slot machines has revived racing attendance, making it more of a destination center, but that's far from general. More commonly, increases in wagering come from viewers in distant simulcast locations once the larger purses enabled by slots begin attracting better horses. Veteran horse players generally prefer betting on quality horses, as they have better odds of consistency.

Better Purses Help

Prairie Meadows spokesman Steve Berry said of on-site track attendance: "That's something we've come to realize was not the point. . . . There's not much crossover with slot machine players and horse players."

The Meadows has seen a 37 percent decline in wagering over the past decade, and attendance is about one-third of what it was, say track officials. The total purse handed out in a day, typically shared in descending order among the top five finishers in each race, has fallen to $45,000 or less from $60,000. At Mountaineer, daily purses averaging $22,000 in the pre-slots days are now $160,000.

Pennsylvania purses will definitely change once the slots are installed. Twelve percent of slots revenue in Pennsylvania will be used to boost the purses. If the slots at the Washington County operation can gross $200 million a year, as officials hope, that would be an extra $24 million annually divided among those connected to the horses.

The Future of Horse Racing

Any surge of general interest in the sport of kings is less certain.

Bill Paulos, a partner in Cannery Casino Resorts, the new owner of The Meadows, said the new facility being designed as a permanent racetrack-casino complex is intended to highlight harness racing as a spectator sport, even for those coming for the slots. As at Presque Isle Downs, restaurant diners will look out through large glass windows onto the track.

"You'd like to get the popularity [of racing] back," said Mr. Paulos, whose background is in casinos rather than racing. "Certainly there's things you can do to try to do that, but it truly is difficult.

"If you look at the average age of a horse player, he's not a young fella. Slots will be a much broader spectrum."

The data on the waning of racing's popularity is not all negative. Although the number of thoroughbred races declined from 72,664 in 1990 to 52,257 by 2005, the amount wagered increased from $9.4 billion to $14.6 billion, according to the Jockey Club, a racing organization. Various forms of off-track betting represent all the growth in horse wagering, and now make up nearly nine of every 10 dollars bet.

Even so, industry analysts say, simulcasting itself might not have sustained horse racing in many locations without the slots to prop up both operators' profits and track purses. Empire City at Yonkers Raceway, in New York's Westchester County, was on its death bed, with no one interested in buying it from Pittsburgh's Rooney family until slots arrived last fall.

Now it has 4,100 machines, with more planned, and it's on a six-day-a-week racing schedule instead of the three or four days it had been running. It's one example of a recently saved track, and probably the most notable.

"What [the addition of slots] has done is buy time for the horse racing part of the industry to be viable, and to try to figure out new ways to attract customers," said Richard Thalheimer, a Kentucky economic consultant on racing and gaming.

But as a night out for entertainment or as a gambling hobby, people have more alternatives to enjoy themselves than during the tracks' heyday decades ago. Those options, of course, include the machines right next door.

Newer forms of gambling, Mr. Liebman noted, "are simpler and more exciting and give more immediate thrills. . . . [Horse betting] takes a longer time, which requires a significant involvement. It's just not the same as pulling a lever or hitting a button or scratching off a lottery ticket."

There's one additional benefit to playing the slots instead of horses: The machines generally return as prize money at least 90 percent of the amount risked, compared to 80 percent for pari-mutuel wagering.

That still averages out to a loss, as the Vasvaris were reminded last week at Mountaineer. Elayne Vasvari stressed, however, she's also walked out hundreds of dollars ahead plenty of times.

"She's more likely to come down here and think she's going to get rich," the white-bearded Ray said with a smiling nod to his upbeat wife. "I come down to relax."

| *"Life on the thoroughbred track is often tantamount to torture for the horses."*

Horse Racing Is Cruel and Dangerous for Horses

Bonnie Erbe

Bonnie Erbe is a radio host and contributing editor to U.S. News & World Report. In the following viewpoint, she views the tragic death of Eight Belles at the 2008 Kentucky Derby as undeniable proof that horse racing is a cruel and brutal sport. Erbe outlines several suggestions to make the sport safer for horses, arguing that we can't call ourselves a civilized society until we ban all forms of animal mistreatment.

As you read, consider the following questions:

1. How does the author describe the Eight Belles tragedy at the 2008 Kentucky Derby?

2. Why does the author believe that new forms of artificial track footing that helps protect horses hasn't been mandated nationwide?

3. How old does the author believe horses should be to race in the United States?

"There is nothing better for the inside of a man than the outside of a horse" is a quote by Winston Churchill often erroneously attributed to Ronald Reagan. But after this weekend's Kentucky Derby, it could be said, "There's nothing worse for the inside or outside of a horse than life on the track."

I've been writing these past few weeks about horrendous and fatal equine accidents in the sport of three-day eventing. I own seven hunter/jumper show horses and maintain my own 40-acre horse farm.

Eventing is much less well known to the public than thoroughbred racing. While artificially difficult courses in that sport take the lives of far too many majestic creatures, statistically the track is much worse. Life on the thoroughbred track is often tantamount to torture for the horses. The slaughter of Eight Belles at Saturday's Kentucky Derby—and I do mean slaughter—should give pause to everyone who ever patronized horse racing. Coming one year after Barbaro's horrid end, Eight Belles' sacrifice should stand as undeniable proof to anyone who ever had doubts about the vicious conditions under which these horses are raised, trained, and forced to race.

The Danger to Thoroughbred Horses

One Jim Squires, identified at the bottom of his article in today's *New York Times* as a thoroughbred breeder, wrote an unusually honest piece about the dangers faced by thoroughbreds:

> . . .the horses we raise are not as sound as they used to be. The thoroughbred horse is one of the most fragile creatures on earth, an animal with a heart and a metabolism too powerful for his bones, digestive and respiratory systems, one too heavy and too strong for the structure supporting it. . . . The concern about the safety of our racetracks is also legitimate. People are trying to do something about that. It is indisputable that more catastrophic injuries occur on dirt

surfaces—too often on the pitifully few days that the world is paying attention to our sport.

There are several things that must be done immediately to spare further equine abuse and death. Mr. Squires touched on some of them, but not all. Yes, new forms of artificial track footing, which have been mandated in California, should be mandated nationwide. Why has this new, more forgiving footing not been put into use everywhere? The answer: money. Since thoroughbreds are no more than money machines for most owners and trainers, these profiteers should be forced to fork over some of their winnings to improve track safety.

Second, the trend toward breeding thinner-boned thoroughbreds should be banned immediately. Horses are bred for speed, which often means thin-boned legs. The thinner the bone, the more easily it breaks. Horses with broken or fractured legs don't always have to be "euthanized" (I prefer the term slaughter, since that's what it really is). They're often killed when owners decline the alternatives: huge veterinary or board bills to keep injured horses standing in hoists for a year or more to allow their bones to heal.

Third, we should ban the racing of 2- and 3-year-olds so popular on the U.S. track. In Europe, horses are typically raced later, when their "growth plates" (leg bones) are fully formed and they are less prone to injury. Greedy Americans don't want to spend the money to keep the horse "hanging around" (to wit, not earning money) until they are 4 or 5 years old, and so we race them before their legs are strong enough to handle injury.

The Horrible Lives of Thoroughbred Horses

Then there's the life these horses have while training to race. The routine I am about to explain is used by some, not all, owners. Care varies greatly from farm to farm and trainer to trainer. I have worked with grooms and farriers who came off the track. The stories they tell are horrifying. They've described how horses are pumped up on "sweet feed" full of processed sugar. Sweet feed in large doses makes horses nervous, violent, even nuts—like kids overdosing on chocolate. But horses are already 1,200 pounds of insanely nervous energy.

Many horses are forced to live 23-7 in their stalls, except for the hour or so per day when they are exercised. The human equivalent would be tying someone to his or her bed for 23 hours per day, only letting them out to run for an hour. Wouldn't you go crazy under those circumstances?

Many track horses are never turned out in pasture or on grass. Horses need large grass pastures to run around. They are herd animals and should be turned out in groups so they can socialize with other horses. Owners and trainers fear horses will get kicked or injured in group turnout. But an isolated horse is like an isolated human: miserable.

Stories of Abuse

While these conditions are bad enough, I have heard stories about sadistic treatment by especially vicious trainers that make your gut spin. One farrier told me he watched while a trainer hobbled a horse (chained together his front and hind feet so he couldn't move), pushed him to the ground and placed him under a tarp in the 90-degree heat. This, so he could break the colt's spirit, because the horse was proving to be difficult to train. This trainer literally tried to "bake" the life out of the colt. He didn't mean to kill him, because that would have cost the owner money. But he did mean to destroy the horse's spirit and to torture him. Others stood by at the track where this took place and did nothing.

Then there are the drugs. Horses are routinely drugged to mask injury and run on damaged muscles or bones. A good friend who used to work on the track once said, "I'd ask my friends why they kept injecting these horses who possessed

ASPCA Statement on the Death of Eight Belles

"The fragile nature of thoroughbred racehorses and the stress and rigors that the industry subjects on these animals is loudly evidenced in the tragic death of Eight Belles who, as we saw, was euthanized after both of her front ankles collapsed just after coming in second at the Kentucky Derby," said ASPCA [American Society for the Prevention of Cruelty to Animals] President & CEO Ed Sayres.

Continued Sayres, "The sport of horse racing is no different than other forms of entertainment where animals are forced to perform, often times in stressful and inhumane conditions. These include being raced too young before reaching physical maturity, being raced excessively, being forced to run on hard or slippery surfaces, or being injected with drugs to enhance performance."

American Society for the Prevention of
Cruelty to Animals (ASPCA), "ASPCA Issues Statement
on Eight Belles' Tragic Death at 2008 Kentucky Derby,"
May 5, 2008.

great breeding? If they were so well bred, why did they have to be shot up with all kinds of drugs to run?"

Learning the Lesson

I hope Eight Belles' death serves as something more than a one-day news story. I hope her sacrifice causes every fan of horse racing to stop patronizing the sport or betting on the mounts until major reforms take place. Congress is now working on legislation to ban horse slaughter in the three remaining slaughterhouses in Texas and Illinois. Canada's animal welfare groups are working to ban slaughter there, too. Horse slaughter should be banned. But so should over-breeding of thoroughbreds, quarter horses, and all types of equines. If horses weren't overbred, we'd treat the smaller number we would have better: how they should be treated, like majesty on legs.

Our society needs to pull back the curtain of secrecy that covers up unforgivable things we allow to happen not just to horses, but to all sorts of animals. Michael Vick's prosecution for dog cruelty was a beginning. But until we ban all animal mistreatment, we have no right to call ourselves civilized or compassionate.

Periodical and Internet Sources Bibliography

The following articles have been selected to supplement the diverse views presented in this chapter.

Scott Bland	"Do State Governments Have a Gambling Addiction?" *Christian Science Monitor*, July 17, 2010.
Boston Phoenix	"Let's Get Serious: Gambling Is Front and Center on Beacon Hill," April 16, 2010.
Ralph R. Caputo and Connie Wagner	"Turning Meadowlands into a Racino Is Common Sense," newjerseynewsroom.com, August 19, 2010. www.newjerseynewsroom.com.
Todd A. Eachus	"Gaming Law Will Help State's Residents and Economy," *Times Leader* (Wilkes-Barre, PA), October 28, 2010.
David R. Francis	"Do Benefits Outweigh the Social Costs of Casinos?" *Christian Science Monitor*, August 30, 2010.
Annette Meeks	"Let's Run the Numbers on Racetracks," StarTribune.com, February 26, 2010. www.startribune.com.
Steven V. Oroho	"Racinos Can Keep New Jersey Green in More Ways than One," newjerseynewsroom.com, July 16, 2009. www.newjerseynewsroom.com.
Bill Sherman	"Odds of Addiction Grow," *Tulsa World*, January 31, 2010.
Tim Shorrock	"Gambling with Biloxi," *The Progressive*, August 2007.
Randy Weidner	"The Public Sees the Value in Racinos," StarTribune.com, March 9, 2010. www.startribune.com.

OPPOSING
VIEWPOINTS®
SERIES

CHAPTER 3

How Should the US Government Treat Online Gambling?

Chapter Preface

In June 2003 the tiny island nation of Antigua and Barbuda brought a controversial case to the World Trade Organization (WTO), the international body responsible for adjudicating trade disputes between countries. Antigua and Barbuda, which is home to a large number of online sports betting and casino operations, charged the United States with unfairly inhibiting US citizens from conducting business with these companies. Arguing that US trade policy did not prohibit cross-border gambling business, Antigua and Barbuda was looking for compensation—they claimed annual damages of $3.44 million—and better access to US markets.

Trade experts noted that Antigua and Barbuda had a valid point. After all, the United States was willing to allow American casino businesses to operate Internet gambling operations overseas; therefore, they should allow foreign-based Internet gambling operations to do business in America. To not allow reciprocal trade was hypocritical on America's part, they contended. They asserted that foreign land-based and Internet gambling operations should have access to the US market, which by some estimates totals more than half the overall global market of online gamblers.

In 2004 the WTO sided with Antigua and Barbuda in its case against the United States, ruling that US laws concerning online gaming were unlawful because the US government allowed American companies to operate online horse-race-betting sites and land-based casinos. The United States responded by passing the Unlawful Internet Gambling Enforcement Act in 2006, which prevents US banks and credit card companies from processing payments to online gambling businesses. This action essentially cut off service to the overseas Internet gambling market.

In 2007 the WTO ruled on the compensation the United States would have to pay: Antigua and Barbuda could violate copyright protections on goods like films and music from the United States worth up to $21 million. That meant that they were allowed to distribute copies of American music, movie, and software products to Antiguan businesses.

The WTO ruling caused a firestorm of controversy in the United States. Critics of the decision charged that the WTO was legitimizing the right to pirate American goods and services. They also argued that the WTO ruling was a direct attack on US sovereignty from an international institution. America, critics contended, should be able to pass laws in its best interest without interference from international bodies. Such meddling could be considered an attack on American economic security, they maintained. Defenders of the decision asserted that the United States had to abide by the decision and fulfill its international obligations.

The debate over the WTO decision is one of the issues touched upon in the following chapter, which concerns the US government's treatment of online gambling. Other issues debated in the chapter concern the impact of the federal ban on Internet gambling and online poker in California.

> *"By passing the Unlawful Internet Gambling Enforcement Act of 2006 Congress was sending a strong message that it was willing both to protect states' prerogatives and to protect families."*

The Federal Ban on Online Gambling Is Warranted

Thomas E. McClusky

Thomas E. McClusky is the vice president for government affairs for the Family Research Council. In the following viewpoint, he observes that overturning the ban on online gambling would be a mistake. McClusky argues that the ban has wide support because there are dire social and financial consequences to allowing Internet gambling, such as crime, divorce, the dissolution of families, bankruptcies, and suicide.

As you read, consider the following questions:

1. According to a study by the National Gambling Impact Study Commission, what are the estimated lifetime costs of gambling for a pathological gambler?

Thomas E. McClusky, "Prepared Testimony Before the U.S. House Judiciary Committee," November 14, 2007.

2. According to the California Council on Problem Gambling, how much do problem gamblers rack up in credit card debt each year?

3. How did the ban impact the number of college students who gambled in 2006, according to a recent study cited in the viewpoint?

Thank you, Mr. Chairman, and all the distinguished Members of the Committee [the House Judiciary Committee] for allowing me to testify today. Part of me was also hoping that former Senator Al D'Amato [R-NY], the well-paid lobbyist for the Pokers Players Alliance, would join us here today [November 14, 2007]. In one of those odd twists of fate the Senator used to play poker with my dad many years ago when they were at Syracuse University together.

However, what the senator and his colleagues lobby for today is very different from the mostly innocent gambling they did back in their youth. In lobbying for legislation such as Congressman [Barney] Frank's bill, H.R. 2046, which seeks to overturn federal and state laws in relation to Internet gambling, and H.R. 2610, sponsored by Representative Robert Wexler (D-FL), which seeks to carve out an exemption for online poker, they seek to open up a Pandora's box of consequences. Adoption of these bills will lead to anonymous corruption, the dissolution of families, and the disruption of today's delicate negotiations between the United States and other countries, notably the United Kingdom and Antigua.

Ban on Internet Gambling Has Broad Support

There are many reasons why Congress decided to take a look at Internet gambling, and it was only after continued prodding from a unique coalition that Congress finally passed the Unlawful Internet Gambling Enforcement Act [UIGEA] of 2006. This coalition's members represented a wide range of

Internet Gambling and the World

Like the United States, a number of other countries have commissioned detailed reviews to determine the implications of gambling, including Internet gambling, within their countries. These countries take a variety of approaches to regulating Internet gambling. For a number of reasons, we were unable to determine how many countries explicitly prohibit Internet gambling. For example, gaming laws in many countries, like those in many U.S. states, apply to gaming in general rather than to Internet gambling. Although we were unable to determine the exact number, an interactive gaming industry services group reported that over 50 countries and foreign jurisdictions, mostly in Europe, the Caribbean, and the Australia/Pacific region, have legalized Internet gambling.

US Government Accountability Office,
"Internet Gambling: An Overview of the Issues," 2002.

support not only from organizations like Family Research Council and Eagle Forum and a host of state family groups, but also from religious organizations such as the United Methodists, Southern Baptists and the National Council of Churches. Every major sports association and many major financial organizations including the American Bankers Association also supported the legislation. They were joined by the National Association of Attorneys General, the National District Attorneys Association, and the Fraternal Order of Police. This deep and diverse support on the federal and state level contributed to a version of the Unlawful Internet Gambling Enforcement Act passing Congress in July of 2006 with a vote of 317–93, and it persuaded the Senate to include the bill in the SAFE Port Act [Security and Accountability for Every Port Act].

Clearly this bill was not some fly-by-night piece of legislation but a well-thought-out measure that was years in the making. For the answer to why such a large and diverse group would gather in support of the UIGEA, one need only look at the National Gambling Impact Study Commission, which was created by Congress in 1996 and issued its final report in 1999. The commission documented the grave toll gambling takes on society. The report estimated that lifetime costs of gambling (including bankruptcy, arrests, imprisonment, legal fees for divorce, etc.) amounted to $10,550 per pathological gambler, and $5,130 per problem gambler. With those figures, it calculated that the aggregate annual costs of pathological gambling caused by the factors cited above were approximately $5 billion, in addition to $40 billion in estimated lifetime costs.

Gambling Has Wide-Ranging Consequences

This financial cost to gamblers in turn affects their families. The report continues that "many families of pathological gamblers suffer from a variety of financial, physical, and emotional problems, including divorce, domestic violence, child abuse and neglect, and a range of problems stemming from the severe financial hardship that commonly results from pathological gambling. Children of compulsive gamblers are more likely to engage in delinquent behaviors such as smoking, drinking, and using drugs, and have an increased risk of developing problem or pathological gambling themselves. As access to money becomes more limited, gamblers often resort to crime in order to pay debts, appease bookies, maintain appearances, and garner more money to gamble."

The aforementioned concerns address gambling as a whole. When you add the anonymity of the Internet, the troubles caused by gambling increase exponentially. The theft of credit card numbers from customers is a very real concern and it is much easier for gambling websites to manipulate games than it is in the physical world of highly regulated casinos. Additionally, gambling on the Internet provides remote access, encrypted data and, most importantly, anonymity. Because of this, a money launderer need only deposit funds into an offshore account, use that money to gamble, lose a small amount of that money, and then cash out the remaining funds.

The Crack Cocaine of the Internet

It is the uniqueness of the Internet when it comes to gambling that inspired Dr. Howard Shaffer, the director of Harvard Medical School's Division on Addictions, to call Internet gambling the "crack cocaine of the Internet" due to the ease with which online gamblers can play from home. Online players can gamble 24 hours a day from home with no real sense of the losses they are incurring. Additionally, while many Internet gambling sites require gamblers to certify that they are of legal age, most make little or no attempt to verify the accuracy of the information. The intense use of the Internet by those under the age of 21 has led to concerns that they may be particularly susceptible to Internet gambling.

Problem gamblers between the ages of 18 and 25 lose an average of $30,000 each year and rack up $20,000 to $25,000 in credit card debt, according to the California Council on Problem Gambling. In a health advisory issued by the American Psychiatric Association in 2001, ten percent to 15 percent of young people reported having experienced one or more significant problems related to gambling.

In September, the British Gambling Prevalence Survey 2007 was published by the National Centre for Social Research. This large, objective government study shows that Internet and electronic forms of gambling are far more addictive than traditional and social forms of gambling. Only 1–2% of Britons who play the lottery are problem gamblers. The study found that 1.7% of people who bet on horse races off-line are problem gamblers, and the rate is about 3% for bingo and slot machines. But compare that with problem gambling rates for people who gamble on computers: 11% for fixed-odds betting terminals (similar to video poker or video lottery terminals in the U.S.), 12% for systems that take spread bets on outcomes ranging from sports to political races to stock prices, 6% for online betting with bookmakers, and 7.4% for other types of online betting, such as online poker. The data is unequivocal: Gambling online is several times more addictive, and regulation of online gambling in Britain doesn't change this fact.

And before I get the question, the rate of problem gambling for "private betting," as in the case of my dad and Senator D'Amato many years ago, is a much lower 2.3%.

The Tragic Consequences for Some Problem Gamblers

In June of this year an aggrieved father, Pastor Greg Hogan Sr. gave powerful testimony to the House Financial Services Committee on how his son, also named Greg—a college student with a bright future ahead of him—became addicted to online gambling. Mr. Hogan told the heartbreaking story of how his son became obsessed with playing poker online and, due to the ease with which it was offered to him (as it is offered to college students across the U.S.), Pastor Hogan's son soon found himself saddled with such deep losses that he turned to bank robbery to pay his debts. Now the main debt Greg Hogan Jr. is paying is to society in the form of a 20-year sentence in federal prison. What Greg Hogan Jr. did was wrong and he is paying for it. However, his family and other families continue to suffer as those they love become obsessed with Internet gambling.

By passing the Unlawful Internet Gambling Enforcement Act of 2006 Congress was sending a strong message that it was willing both to protect states' prerogatives and to protect families. Even before the recent release of the Department of

Treasury's regulations in connection with the UIGEA, Congress's efforts to combat unlawful Internet gambling showed immediate fruit.

A recent National Annenberg Survey [of Youth] study found that the number of college students who gambled in 2006 fell by 70 percent the next year, following the passage of the UIGEA. The new law restricts banks from transferring funds to Internet gambling sites, all of which operate outside the U.S., so many sites closed as a result.

According to Pokerscout.com, a website dedicated to web statistics for online gambling sites, a number of the online gambling operators have stopped accepting bets from players identified to be in the United States and the overall use of these sites has dropped drastically. These losses for online gambling sites are victories for American families; it would be a shame if this Congress decided to reverse the rare strong bipartisanship and rapid progress that have been shown on this important issue.

As I can picture my dad saying to former Senator D'Amato and the questionable alliance behind him, when you have the law, the states, financial institutions, religious and family organizations, and an array of law enforcement agencies against you—it is time to fold your cards and go home.

> "What we do with our own money on our own time ought to be our own business."

The Federal Ban on Online Gambling Should Be Overturned

Radley Balko

Radley Balko is a policy analyst at the Cato Institute. In the following viewpoint, he offers three reasons why the online ban is misguided: the federal government should not be policing our vices and bad habits; it's hypocritical to ban online wagering when states run their own lotteries; and prohibition doesn't work. Balko also notes that no matter the roadblocks Congress puts in their way, gambling companies will find ways to make their services accessible because a healthy market for them exists.

As you read, consider the following questions:

1. According to Balko, how much is spent on Internet wagering?

Radley Balko, "Anti-Gambling Crusade a Bad Bet," Cato Institute, first appeared in *Arizona Republic*, March 12, 2006. Copyright © 2006, Radley Balko. Reproduced by permission of the author.

2. How successful have government attempts been to prevent credit card companies and online payment services from doing business with offshore gaming websites?

3. What effect does the author believe Virginia Representative Bob Goodlatte's antigambling bill will have on gaming companies and offshore financing services?

Online gambling is already illegal in the United States. Proprietors of gaming sites are all incorporated overseas. Yet Internet wagering is still a $12 billion industry.

History has shown us that prohibiting private, consensual behavior has never made that behavior go away. Because consensual crimes take no victims, vice laws are difficult to enforce. Police have to use informers and undercover work and sometimes need to break the very laws they're trying to enforce.

Consequently, America's various attempts at prohibiting sinful behavior have bred corruption, organized crime, black markets and significant erosion of our civil liberties. The story's no different with gambling.

Here are the three chief reasons why Congress's latest vice crusade is misguided:

Feds Not Our Babysitter

What we do with our own money on our own time ought to be our own business. The idea that government is somehow obligated, or even authorized, to protect us from our own vices and "bad" habits simply isn't compatible with a free society.

If five poker enthusiasts want to voluntarily play online, and if a private company wants to provide the technology for that to happen in exchange for a fee, why do members of Congress feel obligated to prevent that from happening?

Like many bad laws, gambling prohibition is often justified in defense of "the children." But for a minor to wager online, he'd need a credit card or access to a bank account. It isn't as if children are easy prey for gambling sites.

It's Naked Hypocrisy

Last month [February 2006], police in Fairfax, Va., conducted a SWAT [Special Weapons and Tactics] raid on Sal Culosi Jr., an optometrist suspected of running a sports gambling pool with some friends. As the SWAT team surrounded him, one officer's gun discharged, struck Culosi in the chest and killed him. In the fiscal year before the raid that killed Culosi, Virginia spent about $20 million marketing and promoting its state lottery.

The scene is similar in other states. Charity and barroom poker games, for example, are being shut down by police departments across the country. Meanwhile, state lotteries are cashing in on the poker craze with Texas Hold'em-style scratch off games.

Congress isn't immune from the double standard. The new antigambling bill sponsored by Virginia Rep. Bob Goodlatte contains a gaping loophole that lets state lotteries continue to sell their tickets online. And just as Goodlatte, Arizona Sen. Jon Kyl and others in Congress have been earnestly lecturing us on why we need our politicians to protect us from our own peccadilloes, 28 states, including Arizona, were cashing in on the hyped $365 million Powerball jackpot.

Which makes all these efforts to ban private gambling sound more like a protection racket than good government.

It Won't Work

As noted, despite prohibitions against Internet gambling, it's still a billion-dollar industry. Prohibitionists have argued that a law preventing credit card companies from allowing their services to be used in conjunction with gaming sites will prove to be the death knell for online wagering.

Hardly. In fact, several state attorneys general already have gone after the credit companies and online payment services

Online poker night, all players have laptops, cartoon by Thomas Bros. www.Cartoon Stock.com.

like PayPal, threatening them with Patriot Act charges for doing business with gaming sites. Consequently, third-party vendors such as Neteller, also located offshore, have sprung up to facilitate transactions between gamers and gaming sites.

Congress can keep passing laws. But so long as there is demand, innovators will continue to use technology to find ways around them.

On CNBC three weeks ago, Goodlatte pointed out that because gambling companies themselves are offshore, they aren't subject to U.S. laws and regulations. But that's an argument against his own bill. Goodlatte's bill won't stop Internet gaming. Instead, it will not only keep gaming companies offshore, it will facilitate the rise of offshore financing services, too.

That means U.S. consumers will be more susceptible to fraud and will have no legal recourse when a shady offshore outfit bilks them out of their money.

Not to mention that offshore, black market outfits present prime funding opportunities for organized crime and international terrorism.

Legalize, Then Regulate Them

A more sensible policy would be to legalize online gambling and let credible gaming companies do business within the reach of U.S. law. The good ones are already begging to be regulated.

They understand that legitimately setting up shop in the United States will give them an advantage over their competitors. Consumers will be more likely to place bets on sites governed by U.S. laws and subject to U.S. courts.

Unfortunately, Congress seems more interested in pushing a moral agenda than taking a realistic approach to a habit that is as old as human nature.

> "As hard as we might try to understand the present United States federal laws on the books when it comes to gambling, and especially with the advent of constantly evolving computer technology, legislation has not kept pace."

US Ban on Online Gambling on Way Out?

Diane M. Grassi

Diane M. Grassi is an investigative reporter. In the following viewpoint, she underlines the flaws in H.R. 2267, which allows Internet gambling if it is licensed and regulated by the US Treasury Department. Grassi finds the bill overly broad and essentially unworkable because none of the government entities tasked with regulatory responsibilities are law enforcement agencies.

As you read, consider the following questions:

1. How much does the federal government estimate in taxable revenue from gambling over a period of ten years, according to Grassi?

2. What would be the role for the US secretary of the treasury under H.R. 2267?

3. According to the viewpoint, is sports betting allowed under H.R. 2267?

When it comes to gambling, there has never been a short-age of opinion amongst the masses. Either people favor it or they feel strongly that it accompanies some of society's more depraved behaviors, along with attracting crime, and is a negative temptation for our youth.

Regardless of what side of the table you are on, most folks can agree that they would like less government regulation when it comes to indulging in their leisure activities of choice. But such becomes far less clear when the government jumps in.

As hard as we might try to understand the present United States federal laws on the books when it comes to gambling, and especially with the advent of constantly evolving com-puter technology, legislation has not kept pace.

Additionally, lawmakers are too often wont to ignore a problem, lest it detract from their popularity, and more im-portantly, when it might interfere with receiving campaign cash from certain lobbying industries.

So they drag their proverbial feet until an issue reaches a fever pitch and it simply must be addressed; even if it is not in a cohesive manner or in the best interests of their constitu-ents.

States Want Online Gambling Revenue

Also, with respect to gambling, I have previously documented in several previously published articles that many state gov-ernments in the U.S. have already started to craft legislation in hopes of feeding their depleted coffers by further relaxing their laws to allow more access to gambling.

Everything from expanding brick and mortar gambling ca-sinos to advancing racinos [a racetrack establishment with slot machines] and adding slot machines at horse race tracks to allowing intrastate and interstate online gambling are seen collectively as a potential bonanza that will cure all ills for the empty tills lining their budgets. And it is estimated by the federal government that there could be as much as a $42 billion windfall over a 10-year stretch in taxable revenue.

It is quite interesting, but not by virtue of coincidence, that most of this seeming rush to pass such legislation by U.S. states comes at the same time that the U.S. Congress is plotting ways to overturn the only recently implemented Unlawful Internet Gambling Enforcement Act of 2006 (UIGEA), through a proposed law by Congressman Barney Frank (D-MA) that he originated in 2009.

It just won its initial approval in the U.S. House of Representatives through its Committee on Financial Services on July 27, 2010, on which Rep. Frank is the chairman. Known as House Resolution 2267 (H.R. 2267) or the Internet Gambling Regulation, Consumer Protection and Enforcement Act, the House Financial Services Committee's approval is but the first phase of its passage, required by both houses of the U.S. Congress.

The Role of UIGEA

In short, the UIGEA was a nice way for the U.S. government to keep offshore online betting casinos at bay from the American consumer. It was initially enacted in October 2006, but was never implemented until June 1, 2010, after many long delays by the federal government's U.S. Department of the Treasury in compelling U.S. banking institutions to honor its rules.

Problems with UIGEA

However, the main problem, which will continue to haunt H.R. 2267, is the actual legal definition of "illegal online gambling," thus creating all kinds of loopholes and wiggle room, from the living room gambler to organized crime, to skirt the law.

And also of concern in the presently active UIGEA is that banks remain the only legally accountable parties subject to penalty and prosecution for furnishing offshore online gambling to U.S. residents, while the U.S. gambler placing the bet remains safe. And to date, banks and payment processors are still unclear as to which transactions are actually required to be blocked.

Due to the difficulty in deciphering a non-finite system for the processing of legal U.S. based online gaming transactions, consumers' credit cards and debit cards cannot only be blocked or frozen, but accounts are often cancelled.

Furthermore, a consumer, ignorant of the UIGEA, could innocently go to a gambling site, not even knowing from where it emanates and later find that their credit line or checking account is in peril, simply by clicking on an illicit site.

So for now, that is the best that the U.S. government has served up, as concerns online gaming. But not shy to outdo itself, even if it compounds a dysfunctional process even more so, the federal government has plans to muck it up again through a poorly framed H.R. 2267; almost immediately setting it up to fail.

Legislation Is Fatally Flawed

H.R. 2267 is overly broad and murky, yet will intrinsically involve the U.S. Department of the Treasury and the U.S. Internal Revenue Service (IRS), amongst other U.S. federal agencies, for starters.

It is merely a wish list without the necessary mechanisms in place to not only generate the hoped for tax revenue, but for enforcing the law itself. And it stands to open the floodgates for illicit online gaming, incongruous with what it should be designed to do.

It would leave online gambling sites left to police themselves, merely under the purview of the U.S. federal government.

And like most other large pieces of U.S. legislation that has been conveniently rushed through to final congressional passage, H.R. 2267 is another boilerplate document of mandates to be fulfilled at a date certain after it is already signed into law.

But due to its ambiguity, which seemingly appears by design, H.R. 2267 calls for provisions and assorted amendments that cover a wide array of issues. And it is worth noting several of them here, in order to show how arduous it will be for its desired compliance.

Why It Won't Work

Firstly, it authorizes the U.S. secretary of the treasury to create a licensing program for regulations and enforcement of the law, issuing licenses to online gambling entities, effective for a period of five years.

Thus, it prescribes the licensing requirements for such Internet gambling entities and prohibits operation of an Internet gambling entity that knowingly accepts bets or wagers from persons within the U.S. without the necessary license issued from the U.S. Department of the Treasury.

The law would prohibit a person, deemed prohibited from gambling with an online gambling entity, from collecting any winnings. Such a system to screen a gambler's veracity must be created by each gambling entity, and to be overseen by the federal government. And such is pure folly at this juncture.

H.R. 2267 would require that an online gambling entity pay required taxes to the IRS. And most curiously of all, each gambling entity, itself, would need to implement safeguards against fraud, money laundering, and terrorist financing.

In addition, each online license would require that gambling sites have strong protections in place to prevent minors

Top Five Global Internet Casino Sites

1. Malta   314
2. Netherlands Antilles   266
3. Canada   255
4. Costa Rica   216
5. Gibraltar   201

Committee on Financial Services,
US House of Representatives, "H.R. 2266,
the Reasonable Prudence in Regulation Act,"
December 3, 2009.

from gambling online, and to prevent inappropriate online advertising targeted to underage gamblers or specifically aimed at compulsive gamblers.

Not only must the gambling site maintain a list of compulsive gamblers, but must block them from site access. And it cannot allow access to its site for those individuals who are delinquent on child support payments. These are just some amongst many other illusory imperatives.

Enforcement of U.S. law for the prevention of and tracking of electronic transactions of funds sent to terrorist organizations abroad has been weak at best through the U.S. Department of the Treasury, nine years since September 11, 2001 [referring to the 2001 terrorists attacks on the United States]. And to essentially require online websites to take on such a task is laughable.

More Unworkable Mandates

Other proposed mandates include that debit cards only be used for transactions, to the exclusion of credit cards. Offshore online gambling operations such as PokerStars.com, FullTiltPoker.com, and UB.com, which allowed U.S. players to access their sites after the UIGEA went into effect, will be

137

banned from acquiring a U.S. license, as well as other entities that intentionally violated this U.S. law.

Each state and Indian tribe may opt out of the federal legislation during the first year after its enactment, requiring that their residents abide by respective local laws.

And sports betting, with the exception of U.S.-based horse racing and pari-mutuel betting, would be disallowed, much to the delight of the professional and college sports industries. U.S. state lotteries, should they eventually become accessible online, would also be exempt.

Freedom Is Illusory

But perhaps falsely anticipated with this new law is the notion that gamblers will be allowed much freedom to do as they wish in the privacy of their own homes. However, given the bevy of requirements for oversight, nothing could be further from the truth. Deadbeat dads need not log on, as previously noted.

But more realistically, beginning with Internet service providers or ISPs, one would expect that they would have to be the gatekeeper for gathering initial information as to whether the gambler is even eligible to gamble, based upon their state of residence, if that state has opted out. And the banks would be the second line of defense, cutting off the gambler's funds if need be, should the online gambling site find that it is a documented compulsive gambler placing the bet.

And should a player gain access to a legitimate site, then the process begins as to whether they are of majority age, has been flagged as a delinquent parent, or has a criminal background. Without such due diligence, the individual gambling site is subject to losing its license.

Certainly none of these entities are law enforcement agencies, so for the federal government to expect legitimate oversight to be realized at these levels seems more than silly.

Smarter Legislation Is Needed

The purpose of this [viewpoint] was to give a glimpse into what lurks ahead for U.S. online gaming and is not intended to disparage the gambling consumer nor the gambling industry. Rather, the intent is to highlight some of the future changes in law which may not best serve the public or the industry.

And contrary to the online gaming industry's millions of lobbying dollars spent in Washington, D.C., in order to help initiate this latest planned legislation, it might be best for it to restrain its glee, at this time.

For one only needs to look at the present economic condition of Las Vegas, NV. It has now been proven, going back to the onset of the current recession in 2008, that the gambling industry is indeed no longer recession proof. Yes, in time Vegas and its hurting East Coast counterpart, Atlantic City, NJ, will both rise again.

However, with a 14.5% unemployment rate that Las Vegas presently owns, it is evidence for when entire economies are dependent upon the gambling industry for the creation of jobs and funding municipal programs, disaster can ensue. Therefore, for entire U.S. state and federal programs' very survival to be based upon discretionary income from gambling has lawmakers living in a fool's paradise.

Hopefully, in the coming weeks and months, prior to the entirety of the U.S. House of Representatives approving H.R. 2267 and before it is sent on to the U.S. Senate, that not only will cooler heads prevail, but that a better proposed outcome will exceed before everyone's chips are cashed in. Cheers!

> *"It is shocking for an unelected foreign tribunal to tell our 435-member House of Representatives, our 100-member Senate, and the president of the United States that they lack the power to protect our people."*

The United States Should Not Allow the World Trade Organization to Interfere in Online Gambling Laws

Phyllis Schlafly

Phyllis Schlafly is a conservative columnist, author, and political analyst. In the following viewpoint, she condemns the World Trade Organization (WTO) decision to award American copyrights and trademarks to Antigua and Barbuda as punishment for US laws prohibiting Internet gambling. Schlafly argues that America has every right to ban Internet gambling and that the WTO should not be able to interfere in American affairs in such a manner.

As you read, consider the following questions:

1. According to the author, what is a piracy permit?

Phyllis Schlafly, "The Outrageous WTO," Eagle Forum, January 9, 2008. Copyright © 2008, Eagle Forum. Reproduced by permission.

2. How many WTO members are required to approve revisions to the conditions under which the United States joined the WTO?

3. Why does Schlafly believe that the WTO decision is a direct attack on US sovereignty?

WTO now stands for World Trade Outrage rather than its original name, World Trade Organization. The WTO just ruled that the Caribbean nation of Antigua and Barbuda can freely violate American copyrights and trademarks in order to punish the United States for our laws prohibiting Internet gambling.

Congress passed the Unlawful Internet Gambling Enforcement Act in 2006 after finding that "Internet gambling is a growing cause of debt collection problems for insured depository institutions and the consumer credit industry." The social and financial costs of gambling would be greatly increased if we permit Internet gambling.

The WTO ordered this punishment because it says U.S. laws interfere with free trade in "recreational services." The foreign tribunal ranks free trade as more important than the intellectual property rights Americans have enjoyed since our Constitution was written.

On Shaky Ground

The WTO's 88-page decision issued in December [2007] contained the panel's remarkable admission that "we feel we are on shaky grounds." But that didn't stop the Geneva tribunal from issuing its ruling anyway.

We have every right as a nation to protect our people against the corruption and loss of wealth that result from gambling on the Internet. It is shocking for an unelected foreign tribunal to tell our 435-member House of Representatives, our 100-member Senate, and the president of the United States that they lack the power to protect our people.

Even American supremacist judges would not have the nerve to authorize stealing copyrights and trademarks as a remedy for one side in an unrelated dispute. But the WTO granted what has been called a "piracy permit" that allows a small Caribbean nation to "pirate," or steal, U.S. property rights.

The response in Washington was to announce an attempt to revise the conditions under which we joined the WTO in 1994. That's a nonstarter because these changes in the WTO treaty would require the approval of all 151 members, most of whom don't like the U.S. anyway.

The WTO's Bias Against the US

The WTO has ruled against the United States in 40 out of 47 major cases, and against us in 30 out of 33 trade remedies cases. After the WTO ruled that the U.S. cannot divert tariff revenue to U.S. companies that are injured by foreign subsidies to their competitors, Vice President Dick Cheney provided the tie-breaking vote in the Senate on December 21, 2005, to kowtow to the WTO.

For many years, opponents of the WTO have predicted that this foreign bureaucracy would massively interfere with our sovereignty. This new ruling is crazy, unjust and impertinent, but without a lot of public protest, it looks unlikely that our "free trade" president or Congress will do anything to protect us from the WTO.

How is a foreign tribunal in Geneva able to put the United States in such a box? It's because the internationalist free trade lobby cooked up a sleazy deal to force the WTO on us back in 1994 during the week after Thanksgiving when Americans were preoccupied with Christmas shopping and festivities.

The deal to lock us into the WTO consisted of three parts. First, the 14-page WTO agreement was surreptitiously added, without debate or publicity, to the 22,000-page revision of the GATT (General Agreement on Tariffs and Trade) implementing legislation, and was voted on under "fast track" rules which allowed no amendments or changes, severely limited debate, and forbade any filibuster.

Second, the Treaty Clause in the U.S. Constitution for ratification of treaties was ignored, and WTO was declared passed by Congress as a non-treaty. Third, the GATT/WTO agreement was passed in the December lame-duck session with the votes of dozens of Congressmen who were looking for lucrative jobs representing foreign interests because they had already been defeated in the Republican landslide of November 1994.

An Attack on US Sovereignty

The WTO is not "free trade" at all, but is a supra-national body in Geneva that sets, manages and enforces WTO-made rules to govern global trade. The WTO includes a one-country-one-vote legislature of 151 nations (we have the same one vote as Cuba), an unelected multinational bureaucracy, and a Dispute Settlement Board which deliberates and votes in secret and whose decisions cannot be appealed or vetoed.

WTO is a direct attack on our sovereignty because it claims it can force us to change our laws to comply with WTO rulings. Article XVI, paragraph 4, states: "Each Member shall ensure the conformity of its laws, regulations, and administrative procedures with its obligations." The WTO has the final say about whether U.S. laws meet WTO requirements.

In this presidential season, the WTO should make easy target practice for any candidate to speak up and defend our sovereignty against the globalists who, under the mantra of "free trade," willingly allow the WTO to tell us what laws we may or may not adopt.

VIEWPOINT 5

> "On a broader level, the U.S. move, if successful, could invite other member nations to buy their way out of their trade commitments."

The United States Should Heed the World Trade Organization Decision on Online Gambling

Lorraine Woellert

Lorraine Woellert is a reporter for BusinessWeek.com. In the following viewpoint, she observes that US attempts to unilaterally decide to exclude Internet gambling from its list of services covered by the World Trade Organization (WTO) were unprecedented and will have negative consequences for American trade relationships. Woellert also notes that US manipulations of the WTO can ultimately lead to other nations trying to renege on trade commitments.

As you read, consider the following questions:

1. According to Woellert, what does Antigua want as reparations for the US online gambling ban?

2. How many other WTO members are seeking unspecified reparations, according to the author?

3. According to the viewpoint, who will decide what economic sanctions the United States will incur because of its actions?

Few paid heed in 2003 when the tiny island nation of Antigua [and] Barbuda started griping about tough U.S. gambling laws. The complaint: Antigua's Internet gambling operations, a major source of jobs for the country, had been hurt because Americans weren't allowed to place bets online.

Four years later, this narrow and almost comical spat has boiled over into a broader dispute involving many of America's top trading partners. What turned up the heat? In May the U.S. unilaterally decided to exclude web gambling from its list of services covered by the World Trade Organization. To do so, it invoked an escape clause in the WTO treaty that allows a country to "modify or withdraw any commitment" to provide open access. This move—almost unprecedentedly—came after the WTO ruled that the U.S. violated trade rules when it blocked "imports" of gambling services from other countries.

But the dispute could be a lose-lose proposition for free trade since the U.S. may have legitimized use of a big loophole in the WTO. Meanwhile an already intense populist American backlash against globalism could be exacerbated by steep sanctions.

The escape clause invoked by the U.S. requires reparations to any WTO members that claim to be hurt by the modified agreement. The diplomats who negotiated the treaty wrote the escape clause in a way that intentionally discouraged its use. The country imposing the trade restriction had to provide "compensatory adjustment" to other countries affected by the change—a vague term that includes the possibility of enormous claims.

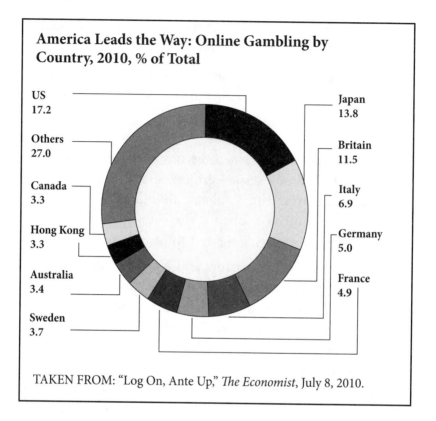

America Leads the Way: Online Gambling by Country, 2010, % of Total

US 17.2

Others 27.0

Canada 3.3

Hong Kong 3.3

Australia 3.4

Sweden 3.7

Japan 13.8

Britain 11.5

Italy 6.9

Germany 5.0

France 4.9

TAKEN FROM: "Log On, Ante Up," *The Economist*, July 8, 2010.

Antigua wants the U.S. to pony up $3.4 billion a year in concessions to cover lost gambling revenues. Seven other WTO members—Japan, India, the European Union, Canada, Australia, Costa Rica, and Macao—are also seeking unspecified but potentially big amends, saying that their web gambling operations, either existing or to be started in the future, have been harmed.

Despite the furor, the U.S. has been unwilling to back away from its aggressive stance on Internet gambling. One reason: It's a rare area where many Republicans and Democrats agree, on both moral and law enforcement grounds. The argument is that it's too easy for minors to gamble online and for criminals and terrorists to use web gambling to launder money. That's why the U.S. beefed up enforcement in recent years and banned the use of credit cards to place online bets.

Moreover, the U.S. says it owes nothing because it never envisioned online betting—or the World Wide Web for that matter—when the trade agreement was signed in 1994. "It never occurred to us that our schedule could be interpreted as including gambling until Antigua and Barbuda brought this case." Deputy U.S. Trade Representative John K. Veroneau told reporters in May.

Ultimately it could fall to the WTO to decide what, if any, economic sanctions the U.S. would incur. Major trading partners such as Europe and Japan could use the case to win concessions in other disputes. Smaller nations, such as Antigua, Costa Rica, and Macao are more likely to ask the WTO to let them ignore copyright protections on software and entertainment. "You could have them be authorized by the WTO to essentially pirate stuff," says Chad P. Bown, an economics professor at Brandeis University.

On a broader level, the U.S. move, if successful, could invite other member nations to buy their way out of their trade commitments. "The last thing we want is for China or India or Russia to feel like they can withdraw some concession on intellectual property or aircraft," says Gary C. Hufbauer, a fellow at the nonprofit Peterson Institute for International Economics in Washington.

Reason could still prevail. The U.S. and Antigua launched formal arbitration proceedings on July 24, and other trading partners have begun bilateral talks. Meanwhile, offshore betting operations are trying to gin up congressional support for legalizing web gambling. If the U.S. doesn't change its laws, "it's going to send a signal to the rest of the world that the WTO is really kind of a one-way street for the benefit of the big economies," says Antigua's lawyer Mark E. Mendel, a partner in the Cork (Ireland) office of Mendel-Blumenfeld. "We're gambling that the U.S. will do the right thing."

"We believe Internet poker will see significant growth when players feel protected by regulations that hold gaming operators accountable to their visitors."

Online Poker in California Should Be Restricted

Robert Martin

Robert Martin is a tribal chairman of the Morongo Band of Mission Indians. In the following viewpoint, he expresses his support for legalizing intrastate Internet poker in California while placing strict regulations on the practice. Martin argues it is essential to have strong consumer protections in place to protect players from fraud and identity theft.

As you read, consider the following questions:

1. According to Martin, how many Californians play online poker each week?

2. How much are Californians wagering per year on the game, according to the viewpoint?

3. Why does Martin believe that intrastate poker must be operated by tribe members?

Robert Martin, Testimony Before California Senate Organization Committee, February 9, 2010.

Thank you for hosting today's informational hearing on Internet poker. The Morongo Band of Mission Indians has been examining Internet poker and its role in the California gaming market for about a year. We appreciate your willingness to explore how the state can address California's booming and unregulated online-poker market. And we want to personally thank you for taking time to study an issue of importance to tribes and to all Californians.

Poker has been popular since the Gold Rush, before California was a state. We recognize Sacramento's jurisdiction over poker, from the days of covered wagons to the Internet highway. There are three points I want to make today about the changing poker market:

1. Player Protections: Regulations are needed. We must adopt consumer protections to safeguard players from fraud, identify theft and cheating by unregulated poker sites.

2. Tax Revenues: Offshore companies are pocketing billions wagered by Californians on Internet poker. That money belongs in California coffers, working for Californians. The state deserves its fair share of that business.

3. Experienced Operators: Trusted Californians—the tribes and licensed card clubs—are the right operators to bring player protections and maximum revenue to the state.

Player Protections

Player protections from fraud, identity theft and cheating must be adopted. Consumer protections are integral to the game of poker. If a customer comes to our casino and does not feel like he is going to get paid, then he's not going to return.

I've had visitors tell me they won't play poker online because they've been cheated or are fearful about security breaches. They don't know who's at the other end of an offshore site. Visa and MasterCard are taking the problem seriously. The two companies are moving to block transactions with illegal Internet gaming operators.

Certainly, technology exists at the state to ensure Internet poker regulations are enforced. The state has been regulating Internet betting on horse races for five years. The popularity of Internet poker exceeds the popularity of racetracks. We believe Internet poker will see significant growth when players feel protected by regulations that hold gaming operators accountable to their visitors.

California's Fair Share

A million Californians a week are playing online poker. They are wagering more than $13 billion a year on the game. They play on sites operated by offshore companies that don't pay taxes and don't generate local jobs. Conservative projections from the Innovation Group have identified $350 million in online poker profits that should be coming to California now. But illegal operators in places like Gibraltar and the Isle of Man are sucking that money out of our state's economy. We must tax online poker as a legitimate source of revenue for the state.

Several states and the federal government are poised to regulate and reap the financial benefits of Internet gaming. The federal government believes it could get as much as $40 billion for the treasury from Internet poker and online gaming. The state must move to get its fair share of this new and growing revenue stream.

Experienced Operators

Online intrastate poker must be operated by Californians in California. Tribes have been running successful brick-and-mortar poker games for 25 years. Card clubs have been operating poker in California for many decades. We have established expertise in the business.

In just 25 years, Morongo's gaming business has flourished from a tiny bingo hall on the side of Interstate 10 to a mega-resort and casino.

We know gaming. We are accountable to our customers. We are invested in our communities. We create jobs. We pay taxes. At the Morongo Casino, we have developed in-house programs and educational tracks so employees who are running drinks can advance and learn to run a casino. As a result, we have developed outstanding and ethical business leaders who've worked their way into the ranks of upper management in the state's gaming industry.

We have broad support in our communities. Tribes and the card clubs are committed to our local, regional and state economies. We are Californians. We want what is best for California.

Exclusivity

Internet poker is a class II game. It does not imperil tribal compacts with the state of California. The California [Office of] Legislative Counsel came to the same conclusion in 2008. I would like to introduce our attorney, George Forman, to speak to the committee on this topic.

Protecting Californians

State lawmakers must adopt regulations and consumer protections to safeguard Californians from fraud and abuse by off-shore Internet poker operators.

Taxing Internet poker will generate a revenue stream for state coffers while offering California consumers the protections they deserve. Tribes and licensed card clubs are perfectly poised to operate legitimate Internet poker play in California.

A few years ago, we had a million-dollar promotion at the Morongo Casino. We thought we had a winner. Two sevens dropped. Another seven hung briefly before it fell. The place went wild. Everyone on the floor thought we had a winner.

We didn't. We had a malfunction. There was discussion about what should be done. The issue came to the tribal council.

We paid out.

We want our customers to know we are on their side. The Morongo tribe will offer the same consumer protections to Internet poker players as we do to the customers who take a seat at our tables.

Allow tribes and the card clubs the opportunity to offer consumer protections on legitimate Internet poker sites. Californians will thank you for protecting them and for strengthening the state's economy by regulating and taxing Internet poker play.

Let's do what's best for consumers.

Let's do what's best for California.

Let's regulate and tax Internet poker and get the state its fair share.

*"Sometimes it is better to be uncertain
of your legal standing than to know
that an activity you enjoy has become
a criminal offense."*

Online Poker Should Not Be Restricted in California

Michelle Minton

Michelle Minton is the director of insurance studies at the Competitive Enterprise Institute. In the following viewpoint, she points out that California's proposed bill, SB 1485, supposedly legalizes Internet gambling for residents, but the law really only legalizes it at the three online gambling platforms—it would be criminalized at any other venue. Minton finds these restrictions to be "offensive to defenders of individual rights, open markets, or personal privacy."

As you read, consider the following questions:

1. Is poker considered an unlawful Internet gambling activity in California, according to Minton?

2. According to the author, how many online games has California made illegal currently?

Michelle Minton, "CA to Criminalize Internet Poker?" OpenMarket.org, June 29, 2010. Copyright © 2010, OpenMarket.org, a Project of the Competitive Enterprise Institute. Reproduced by permission.

3. Under the proposed law, will Californians be able to
gamble at the online sites they want to illegally?

That is, unless you play at one of the three state-sanctioned
"hubs."

Much like other proposals to "legalize" online poker and
other Internet gambling activities, proposals to legalize on a
limited basis such as the proposed SB 1485 in California, seem
like a step forward to online poker players who, for many
years, have wagered money on the Internet in a legal gray
area. But sometimes it is better to be uncertain of your legal
standing than to know that an activity you enjoy has become
a criminal offense.

After the UIGEA [Unlawful Internet Gambling Enforcement Act] was passed in 2006, as I have written about in the
past, it was thought that online gambling would soon be officially criminalized. But when the final rule came down and
the implementation date arrived (the day when all banks and
credit processing companies needed to abide by the new rules),
poker players realized that not much had changed in their experience of online play.

However, during the interim between UIGEA's passage and
the implementation of its watered-down version, a few legislators initiated bills to legalize certain online gambling activities,
both federally and locally in their home states.

Criminalizing Poker in California

Making news these days is California's latest attempt, initiated
by Sen. Rod Wright [who] introduced SB 1485, a bill that
supposedly legalizes Internet gambling for residents. What it
would actually do is legalize gambling only at the three online
platforms and criminalizes Internet poker played anywhere
else online. Currently, there are no federal laws that make online poker games a crime and the DOJ [Department of Jus-
tice] has never prosecuted individual players associated with

How Much Revenue Could Actually Be Generated in California?

Our analysis indicates that the actual level of state revenue that could be generated from authorizing online poker in California would depend heavily on a variety of factors. These factors include:

- Possible legal issues regarding tribal-state compacts.

- How legal poker websites would be implemented in California.

- The number of people that would play online poker, as well as the amount wagered, on legal websites.

- The extent to which the legal websites are able to capture monies that are currently being wagered on illegal websites.

Legislative Analyst's Office,
"Authorization of Online Poker in California,"
February 9, 2010.

the activity. California makes 11 named games illegal to play online, but poker is not one of them. Thus, in CA, poker is not considered an unlawful Internet gambling activity at the moment. But if a law is passed that sanctions only three online providers, chosen by the state, as SB 1485 does, then playing poker online anywhere else will be a crime. The state's DOJ will be allowed to arrest any individual caught playing poker online at a non-sanctioned site.

Currently, California law makes 11 named games illegal to play online or any game where the operator takes a rake (a cut of the money won in each hand). Thus, online poker in the state is legal at the moment.

Problems with the Bill

This type of restricted legalization is, not only offensive to defenders of individual rights, open markets, or personal privacy, but also it just will not work or do what Wright and proponents hope it will.

1. First, it will not add protections for consumers because gamblers will continue to operate at non-sanctioned sites.

The text of the proposed regulations recognizes that "millions of Californians" gamble at online casinos for money. Once there are a handful of state-sanctioned casinos, Californians will continue to play at the online sites that they are familiar with or that court their business.

2. It pushes gambling further into the shadows.

If the senator is concerned about these millions of gambling Californians, he should be aware that criminalizing their chosen activity will not accomplish this goal. Rather, it simply pushes them further into the shadows. Any player who is defrauded or robbed in an online game might be too afraid to speak with authorities, lest he be charged with the misdemeanor offense of playing a game online.

3. There is no way to prevent people from continuing to gamble at the online sites they want to.

Much like the UIGEA before it, this type of limited access is impossible without some other major intrusion on personal privacy (such as monitoring a person's computer activity). Online casinos in other states or other countries will continue to serve Californians.

4. The flow of money into the state's coffers will not increase.

Sure, criminalizing an activity adults engage in freely and that violates no other person's rights is a massive breach of regulatory authority, but it won't even increase tax revenue for California. The gamblers who play online now will continue to play unlawfully, and have greater incentive *not* to report income earned online. Add in the cost of enforcement and licensing the three sanctioned hubs and the final tally may end up costing Californians more money than it brings in.

With the state's massive deficit, the promise of millions in new revenue might convince others that this is a good idea. My advice, as it often is when it comes to the Golden State, is that gamblers or anyone else who likes to make decisions about their own life, might consider moving to Nevada.

Periodical and Internet Sources Bibliography

The following articles have been selected to supplement the diverse views presented in this chapter.

Radley Balko	"The Internet Gambling Ban," *Reason*, January 3, 2008.
Les Bernal	"A Predatory Business," *New York Times*, July 29, 2010.
Sewell Chan	"Congress Rethinks Its Ban on Online Gambling," *New York Times*, July 28, 2010.
Christian Science Monitor	"Bill to Legalize Internet Gambling: No Dice," July 23, 2010.
Christian Science Monitor	"Don't Fold on Internet Gambling Ban," March 25, 2008.
Lisa Fabrizio	"Mary Poppins Gone Mad," *American Spectator*, July 19, 2006.
Robert Hahn	"Leveling the Playing Field," *New York Times*, July 29, 2010.
John Kindt	"Keep the Ban," *New York Times*, July 29, 2010.
Las Vegas Review-Journal	"Internet Gambling Ban Under Pressure," September 13, 2007.
Eli Lehrer and Michelle Minton	"No Dice," *American Spectator*, March 25, 2008.
Michelle Minton	"Legalizing Online Gambling Is a No-Brainer," Forbes.com, December 9, 2010. www.forbes.com.
Koleman Strumpf	"Online Gambling Ban Doomed to Fail," FoxNews.com, February 19, 2004. www.foxnews.com.

CHAPTER 4

What Are the Effects of Online Gambling?

Chapter Preface

One of the main objections to Internet gambling in the United States is that the practice leads to gambling addiction. Critics charge that it would attract a whole new population of gamblers who do not want to—or are too young to—go to traditional gambling venues, like casinos or racinos. Furthermore, detractors claim, Internet gambling is hard to monitor and could be a pathway to financial ruin for those not emotionally or mentally prepared for the temptations of gambling. Opponents of the practice vehemently argue against legalizing it out of a good faith attempt to protect the most vulnerable of Americans: the borderline gamblers, children and teenagers, and the financially strapped. As Larry Ashley, a gambling addiction specialist, wrote in a 2010 *New York Times* debate on Internet gambling: "People are already addicted to the Internet—checking e-mails constantly, obsessing over games of solitaire. Gambling is widely available in America. Why add online options when we know how destructive this vice can be?"

Supporters of Internet gambling contend that we need to weigh the social costs of gambling against the potential economic benefits for American businesses. They concede that there is a marked danger of children and teenagers becoming pathological gamblers, but point out that US citizens already have access to gambling, both legal and illegal. Teenagers can already find dozens of venues to place bets or play poker if they are motivated to do so, advocates assert. In fact, supporters argue, legalization of online gambling can actually help problem gamblers by putting in place effective regulation on the practice to protect individuals, especially children and teenagers. Another benefit of legalization, they reason, would be the revenue gained from American Internet gambling businesses, a significant factor in the midst of a depressed economy.

Another argument against online gambling prohibition is that bans simply do not work. As illustrated by earlier prohibitions against alcohol and drugs, people who want to participate in banned activities find a way to do so. As Michelle Minton observes in a 2010 *New York Times* debate, "Instead of legalizing a limited number of online gambling activities and a few online casinos who can jump through the right hoops, we ought to repeal any kind of gambling ban and make it easier for platforms to comply with existing laws and for players to report earnings. This is the best option, not only for revenue generation, but for consumer protection and individual liberty."

The debate over the effects of online gambling is explored in the following chapter. Other viewpoints discuss a ban on online gambling as a violation of American civil liberties and accusations that Internet gambling is unregulated and dangerous.

| *"In fact, the negative consequences of online gambling can be more detrimental to the families and communities of addictive gamblers than if a bricks-and-mortar casino was built right next door."*

Online Gambling Is Harmful

Bob Goodlatte

Bob Goodlatte is a Republican congressman from Virginia. In the following viewpoint, he asserts that the consequences of online gambling for gamblers, their families, and their communities are pernicious and require the cooperation of state and federal governments to adequately and effectively combat them. To that end, Goodlatte argues that recent attempts to legalize online gambling are ill-advised.

As you read, consider the following questions:

1. According to the viewpoint, what is the Federal Wire Act?

2. How many attorneys general signed a letter to Congress calling for legislation to combat Internet gambling?

Bob Goodlatte, "Establishing Consistent Enforcement Policies in the Context of Online Wagers," in House Judiciary Committee, US House of Representatives, November 14, 2007.

3. According to the Annenberg Public Policy Center, how much has card playing for money among college-age youth declined from 2006 to 2007?

Contrary to what many in the gambling community would lead you to believe, gambling is not a victimless activity. In fact, the negative consequences of online gambling can be more detrimental to the families and communities of addictive gamblers than if a bricks-and-mortar casino was built right next door.

The anonymity of the Internet makes it much easier for minors to gamble online. Furthermore, online gambling can result in addiction, bankruptcy, divorce, crime, and moral decline just as with traditional forms of gambling, the costs of which must ultimately be borne by society. In fact, I have been contacted by a constituent in my district whose son fell prey to an Internet gambling addiction. Faced with insurmountable debt from Internet gambling, he took his own life. Unfortunately, financial ruin and tragedy are not uncommon among online bettors.

Traditionally, states have had the authority to permit or prohibit gambling that occurs wholly within their borders. Indeed, state gambling laws vary greatly with states like Nevada permitting and regulating virtually all gambling and states like Utah prohibiting virtually all forms of gambling.

The Trouble with the Internet

With the development of the Internet, however, state prohibitions and regulations governing gambling have become increasingly hard to enforce as electronic communications move freely across borders. Many gambling operations are beginning to take advantage of the ease with which communications can cross state lines in order to elicit illegal bets and wagers from individuals in jurisdictions that prohibit those

Do You Have a Gambling Problem?

- Did you ever lose time from work or school due to gambling?

- Has gambling ever made your home life unhappy?

- Did gambling affect your reputation?

- Have you ever felt remorse after gambling?

- Did you ever gamble to get money with which to pay debts or otherwise solve financial difficulties?

- Did gambling cause a decrease in your ambition or efficiency?

- After losing did you feel you must return as soon as possible and win back your losses?

- After a win did you have a strong urge to return and win more?

- Did you often gamble until your last dollar was gone?

- Did you ever borrow to finance your gambling?

- Have you ever sold anything to finance gambling?

- Were you reluctant to use "gambling money" for normal expenditures? . . .

Most compulsive gamblers will answer yes to at least seven of these questions.

Gamblers Anonymous, "Twenty Questions," 2010.

activities. The most egregious types of these operations are those overseas operations that have little fear of violating U.S. and state laws.

Congress has acted in this area before. In 1961 Congress passed the Federal Wire Act [also known as the Interstate Wire Act] which cracked down on illegal gambling operations that were using telephone lines to communicate bets and wagers across state lines in violation of state law. This statute was passed to help states enforce their own gambling laws, and was cutting-edge at the time. However, today the Internet and wireless technologies are the preferred method of communicating illegal bets and wagers across state lines and we needed to make sure the law contemplates Internet transactions, as well as traditional wire communications.

Pulling Together to Deal with the Threat

Virtually all state law enforcement agencies support federal laws to give teeth to their gambling laws. Last Congress, 48 attorneys general signed a letter to Congress calling for legislation to combat Internet gambling. The letter declared that "We, the undersigned Attorneys General, wish to express our strong support for the efforts of the 109th Congress to pass legislation seeking to combat illegal Internet gambling in the United States. While we do not support federal preemption of our state laws related to the control of gambling, Internet gambling transcends state and jurisdictional boundaries and requires that all segments of the law enforcement community (state, federal and local) work together to combat its spread."

The Department of Justice [DOJ] has consistently stated publicly that it believes that the Wire Act covers Internet technologies and also covers all forms of gambling. However, DOJ has also welcomed legislation to clarify these provisions in order to allow it to more efficiently prosecute violations. One only has to look as far as the prosecutions of the payment processing company Neteller and the Internet gambling site BetonSports to see that DOJ can and does aggressively and effectively enforce the laws.

Legislative Attempts to Combat Internet Gambling

In order to provide more tools to law enforcement, the House of Representatives passed H.R. 4411 last Congress by an overwhelming bipartisan vote of 317–93. This legislation was perhaps the strongest legislation prohibiting Internet gambling that has been considered on the House floor in the past few decades. It contained important provisions to update the Wire Act, including clarifying that it covers all forms of gambling as well as all forms of technology that allow interstate gambling activities to occur. This legislation also contained important provisions to give law enforcement an additional tool to prohibit illegal Internet gambling, namely, it required financial transaction providers to block payments of illegal bets and wagers. This legislation was the subject of hearings and markups in the Judiciary and Financial Services Committees, as well as robust debate on the House floor.

Ultimately, only the portion of the bill blocking illegal Internet gambling payments was signed into law. In keeping with previous laws, the new law only applies to transactions that violate state and federal gambling laws, thus continuing to leave the decision of whether to allow or prohibit gambling primarily with the states.

Efficacy of the New Law

While it was only one piece of the broader House-passed bill, this new law, coupled with stepped-up enforcement actions by DOJ, has already proven extremely effective. A new study by the Annenberg Public Policy Center shows that card playing for money among college-age youth has declined from 16.3% in 2006 to 4.4% in 2007. The same study shows that weekly use of the Internet for gambling among the same age bracket has declined from 5.8% in 2006 to 1.5% in 2007. Perhaps even more promising is the fact that problem-gambling symptoms have declined since last year. Among males ages 18–22, those who reported some type of gambling on a weekly basis and who also reported at least one symptom of problem gambling dropped from 20.4% in 2006 to 5.9% in 2007.

The Department of Treasury has issued draft regulations implementing the antigambling statute we passed last Congress, and it is my understanding that there will be a witness in the next panel to explain in detail the proposed regulations.

While there was overwhelming bipartisan congressional support for a strong ban on Internet gambling in the House just last year, that has not stopped many in Congress from introducing legislation this year to overturn and even reverse the new federal statute, including legislation to override all state laws and permit all Internet gambling at the federal level and legislation to exempt poker and other forms of gambling from the definition of bets and wagers in the law. These types of bills are premature at best since the regulations have not even been finalized yet. At worst, these bills have the potential to reverse the positive trend mentioned above of reducing addictive behaviors that destroy the lives, families, and financial well-being of America's citizens.

"In any case, it's plain that one cannot safely draw any conclusions about the usual experience of online gamblers from the story of the minister's son who robbed a bank to support his poker habit."

The Danger of Online Gambling Has Been Sensationalized

Jacob Sullum

Jacob Sullum is a senior editor at Reason *magazine and Reason .com and a nationally syndicated columnist. In the following viewpoint, he observes that anti-online gambling activists often use prohibitionist logic, which says "anything that can be done to excess should be illegal"—a logic that can also be applied to shopping, drinking alcohol, eating, and sex. Sullum contends that studies show that there isn't a serious online gambling problem and notes for the broad majority of people online poker is a pleasurable hobby.*

As you read, consider the following questions:

1. According to a 2006 study by the *American Journal of Psychiatry*, what percentage of shoppers experience "compulsive buying"?

2. According to a 2007 United Kingdom study, what percentage of people who had placed sports bets online qualified as "problem gamblers" based on American Psychiatric Association criteria?

3. According to champion poker player Annie Duke, how much does the average online poker player spend per week?

Annie Duke, who testified at a recent House Judiciary Committee hearing on Internet gambling, is not a typical poker player. A professional for 13 years, she is the biggest female money winner in the history of tournament poker.

Gregory J. Hogan Jr. is not a typical poker player, either. As his father, the pastor of the First Baptist Church in Barberton, Ohio, explained at a House Financial Services Committee hearing last summer [2007], "Gregory Jr. is currently in prison for a robbery he committed to feed his online gambling addiction."

While Annie Duke recognizes that most Americans who play poker do it for fun, not for a living, Pastor Hogan tends to overgeneralize from his son's equally extreme experience with the game, which involved losing hundreds of dollars a day while playing 12 hours at a time. Hogan demands an addict's veto over Internet gambling: Because his son robbed a bank, he thinks, no one should be allowed to play poker online.

"I oppose any effort to legalize or even give credibility to Internet gambling," Hogan said. He called last year's passage of the Unlawful Internet Gambling Enforcement Act, which effectively requires American financial institutions to shun

History of Internet Gambling

The idea of using the Internet for betting is not new. Donald Davies, a British computer scientist and co-inventor of the packet-switching technology that drives data transmission over the Internet, first proposed using that technology for wagering in December 1965. The first commercial online gambling sites appeared in the mid-1990s, offering casino games and sports books. Online poker followed a couple of years later.

"Log On, Ante Up," The Economist, *July 8, 2010.*

transactions related to online wagers, "an answer to my prayers that other families would not have to suffer as my family has."

Prohibitionist Logic Does Not Apply

Hogan's argument is a fine illustration of prohibitionist logic, which says anything that can be done to excess should be illegal. But as Duke noted, "If the government is going to ban every activity that can lead to harmful compulsion, the government is going to have to ban nearly every activity. Shopping, day trading, sex, (eating) chocolate, even drinking water—these and myriad other activities, most of which are part of everyday life, have been linked to harmful compulsions."

According to a survey reported in the October 2006 *American Journal of Psychiatry*, about 6 percent of shoppers experience "compulsive buying." Data from the federal government indicate that the rate of alcohol abuse or dependence among past-year drinkers is something like 13 percent.

By comparison, a 2007 government-sponsored survey in the United Kingdom, where Internet wagering is legal, found that 6 percent of people who had placed sports bets online and 7.4 percent of people who had placed other kinds of online bets in the previous year qualified as "problem gamblers" based on American Psychiatric Association criteria. That does not mean they were robbing banks; it means they acknowledged at least three of 10 gambling-related problems, such as "chasing losses," "a preoccupation with gambling," "a need to gamble with increasing amounts of money" and "being restless or irritable when trying to stop gambling."

The prevalence of problem gambling among all past-year gamblers (excluding lottery ticket buyers) was 1.3 percent. Does that mean "gambling online is several times more addictive" than other forms of gambling, as Thomas [E.] McClusky of the Family Research Council claimed at the House Judiciary Committee hearing?

Not necessarily. It could simply be that people who are inclined to gamble heavily are especially attracted to online gambling. Notably, the overall rate of problem gambling in the United Kingdom remained unchanged between 1999 and 2007, despite the rise (and legalization) of Internet wagering.

Focusing on Worst Cases Is Unproductive

In any case, it's plain that one cannot safely draw any conclusions about the usual experience of online gamblers from the story of the minister's son who robbed a bank to support his poker habit. According to Duke, the average online poker player spends about $10 a week, in exchange for which he has some fun and sharpens his skills.

"For the majority of Americans, playing poker is a hobby," Duke told the House Judiciary Committee. "They should have a right to choose how to spend their discretionary income, whether it be on poker or anything else." They do not expect to become poker champions, and they should not be treated like bank robbers.

> *"And I will remind anyone who is interested in this subject that it is the states and the people of the states, adults in those states, who have gone to the polls or their legislative representatives have passed laws saying that illegal Internet gambling should be stopped."*

The Government Has a Right to Protect Citizens from Predatory Businesses

Spencer Bachus

Spencer Bachus is a Republican congressman from Alabama. In the following viewpoint, he maintains that American society ought to protect its youth by banning Internet gambling, which he views as a predatory business. Bachus also reinforces the fact that it was state attorneys general who asked for help against Internet gambling and that the American people want the practice stopped.

As you read, consider the following questions:

1. According to Bachus, how is online gambling unique?

Spencer Bachus, "H.R. 2266, the Reasonable Prudence in Regulation Act; and H.R. 2267, the Internet Gambling Regulation, Consumer Protection, and Enforcement Act," in Committee on Financial Services, US House of Representatives, December 3, 2009.

2. Why does the author believe that young people are particularly at risk?

3. How many House members voted for the ban on online gambling, according to the author?

I think, as all of us know, Chairman [Barney] Frank and I have very different views on this, and we approach this very differently. He wants to legalize Internet gambling, and then he wants to tax it. On the other hand, I believe that Internet gambling is and has been and will continue to be a substantial threat to our youth, and that any economic benefit from taxing Internet gambling would be more than offset by the harm it causes our young people.

And we have had hearing after hearing where experts testified as to really what we have as a wave of young Americans who are addicted to gambling and the problems that causes, which are in many cases heartbreaking. I saw an article in the *New York Times* where one mother wrote a letter to the editor describing the horror that had been created from her son whom she basically has lost to Internet gambling.

The Dangers of Online Gambling

Internet gambling characteristics are unique. Online players can gamble 24 hours a day, 7 days a week from home. Children may play without sufficient age verification, and they can bet with a credit card. We have had testimony before that this undercuts a player, particularly a young person's perception of the value of cash; that the younger you become engaged in this behavior, the more addictive it is. It actually wires the brains of some of our young people. It leads to addiction, bankruptcy, and crime. We have actually had testimony that one of the most outstanding young football players from a Florida university, his whole career was ruined, and that career started with Internet gambling at a young age. He, in fact, was arrested for burglarizing a business to pay for gambling debts.

Young people are particularly at risk because if you put a computer in a bedroom or a dorm room of a young person, it is a temptation that many fall prey to. It is simply asking too much of young people that they resist this temptation.

A Responsibility to Protect America's Youth

The chairman talks about America and what it stands for, and one of the things it stands for is not telling adults what they can and cannot do. But one thing that America also stands for, and I think every society, whether it is American society or any other society, I think one of our number one goals ought to be protecting our youth. We certainly do not allow people to come into their bedroom and serve them liquor at a young age or sell them pornography. And the fact that the chairman says, well, you know, you can buy pornography on the Internet, you can order liquor on the Internet, you ought to be able to allow Internet gambling, I think makes no sense whatsoever.

For more than a decade, the majority of this Congress has worked for and voted for legislation to combat illegal Internet gambling. It has always been illegal in the United States, but no one could enforce the law because these criminal enterprises operated offshore. They operated offshore because that removed them from the long arm of not only the Justice Department, but also other law enforcement agencies.

The American People Want Online Gambling Banned

We have had letters from the great majority of attorneys general telling us that without some legislation such as the legislation that we passed in 2006, they were powerless to stop Internet gambling, which was against the law of all their states.

And I will remind anyone who is interested in this subject that it is the states and the people of the states, adults in those states, who have gone to the polls or their legislative representatives have passed laws saying that illegal Internet gambling should be stopped. The states prohibit it, and the last time I looked, all of them did it through a democratic process.

In a nation of law, it only makes sense to try to put these illegal Internet criminal enterprises out of business and not reward them as the chairman would do. Congress took a major step towards protecting our youth and stopping this illegal activity with the passage of the 2006 Unlawful Internet Gambling Enforcement Act. It is that act that the chairman continues to try to repeal or postpone enactment of, and obviously he has allies at the Treasury Department and the Federal Reserve who last week [late November 2009] announced that they were again delaying implementation of the law another 6 months. These regulations should have been finalized and implemented more than 2 years ago. This Congress voted; the House voted by an overwhelming number, over 330 members, as I recall, over three-fourths of the Congress, to stop illegal Internet gambling. And, Mr. Chairman, I think it is time for you, the Treasury, and the Fed to stop delaying the will of the great majority of this Congress and the American people. Quit the foot dragging and enforce this law.

"My quarrel is with people who, thinking that gambling is wrong, want to prevent other people from doing it."

The Online Gambling Ban Is an Encroachment on Civil Liberties

Barney Frank

Barney Frank is a Democratic congressman from Massachusetts and the former chairman of the House Committee on Financial Services. In the following viewpoint, he contends that an online gambling ban crosses the line of government regulation—adults should be able to decide for themselves how to spend their own money without the threat of imprisonment hanging over their heads. Frank also argues that making protecting children and teenagers a priority does not mean that those prohibitions should also be placed on adults.

As you read, consider the following questions:

1. What book does Frank recommend that reflects on the role of government?

Barney Frank, "Can Internet Gambling Be Effectively Regulated to Protect Consumers and the Payment System?" Committee on Financial Services, US House of Representatives, June 8, 2007.

2. Why does Frank reject the argument that we must ban online gambling to protect poor people?

3. What does Frank say about the link between online gambling and terrorism?

This hearing [of the House Committee on Financial Services in June 2007] is on the subject of the regulation of Internet gambling. Gambling in general is not the jurisdiction of this committee, and in fact, I had a conversation on Monday [June 4, 2007], I believe of this week, or Tuesday, rather, with John Conyers, the chairman of the Judiciary Committee, which has primary jurisdiction over gambling.

In the previous Congress, we did enact legislation to restrict the payment of Internet debts where credit cards were involved, and that's wholly within our jurisdiction. I voted against that bill, and I think it's important to be clear about what I think is really at issue here.

The Real Issue Is Moral Objections

The bill was justified in part by people who said that we must prevent money laundering for the purposes of either terrorism or drugs, and that we must prevent young people from doing things that they shouldn't do. But my own conviction, having talked to a lot of members, and listening to the debate, is that the primary motivation came from people who think gambling is wrong.

Now, I have no quarrel with people who think that gambling is wrong. My quarrel is with people who, thinking that gambling is wrong, want to prevent other people from doing it.

This whole debate has driven me back to a book that I only vaguely remembered, and I have now become impassioned with: John Stuart Mill's *On Liberty*. I recommend it to people for the great philosophic text in our tradition.

The Wisdom of *On Liberty*

The book makes the essential point that it is not the role of the government to send people with guns, under the threat of imprisonment, to make you better. We can give people infor-mation. We can, through various institutions in the society, give people instruction. But in the end, adults ought to be able to decide for themselves how they will spend the money that they earn themselves, as long as it does not have an effect on others.

Now, it is possible to argue that everything we do affects everybody else. People have said, "Well, you say it doesn't af-fect others, but if you gamble too much, then you're affecting others." Well, if you do anything too much, it affects others. The problem with that is it's a classic case of an argument that proves too much.

If you take that argument that, in fact, people have a right to your services, that people have a right for you to be healthy, it goes to extremes. People start telling each other what to eat, when to exercise; all of those things affect you.

Drawing the Line

Clearly, there is in the minds of most of us a distinction be-tween those things we do that primarily affect ourselves and those who choose voluntarily to associate with us, and those things that we do that inevitably impact on others. That is a line that I think government would be well advised to respect, and this bill undoes that.

It is one of the rare cases where some of my conservative friends and some of my liberal friends come together. I have conservative friends who tell me gambling is wrong, and ap-parently I hear from some that there are biblical injunctions against it, although apparently there is an exception for bingo, which I have not yet been able to—I don't have a good enough textual expertise to find it, but I gather it is there. On the part of my liberal friends, to be honest, I think many of them think it's tacky. I think that they just don't think it's a nice thing to do, and therefore feel free to ban other people from doing it.

Some argue, well, we must protect the poor from spending their money unwisely. I reject that. If you want to help poor people, there are other ways to do it.

The Freedom to Act Foolishly

I suppose if you don't have enough money, there are a lot of things that I might advise you not to do: drink beer; go to baseball games; buy certain things; or spend too much on articles of clothing. Yes, there are a lot of pieces of advice we should give people. But I would not legally ban lower-income people from spending too much on their athletic shoes and their jeans, and I don't think we should do that here.

Protecting Children

Now, I know the argument is, well, but there are abuses here. I believe we can deal with the abuses. Let me deal with one, and that is young people. There is a great danger in this society that we will substantially circumscribe the freedom that adults ought to have because we are afraid that some young people might abuse it.

It is incumbent upon us to try to differentiate in our laws between what adults can do and young people can do, and as far as Internet is concerned, I will say, from a lot of my conservative colleagues, I hear the mantra, "Never regulate the Internet."

And I guess what they really mean is, "Never regulate the Internet unless we find something offensive, and then we'll regulate it," because this is the most substantive interference with the freedom of the Internet that has ever been enacted into law.

People are entitled to be for this. They are not entitled to be for this and then say, "Oh, but we respect the integrity of the Internet to be free."

And let me just close by saying this: We do allow a number of things to go on through the Internet that should be age restricted. You can buy wine over the Internet. You can buy cigarettes over the Internet. You can look at—in fact, the courts have said to us, to the Congress, "You have gone too far in terms of First Amendment rights in banning certain kinds of sexual-oriented material." Instead, they have said, "Differentiate according to age."

So we have been told by the courts, by the Supreme Court of the United States, that it is not appropriate simply to ban something entirely because young people might abuse it. Instead, we are under the obligation constitutionally to do the best we can to differentiate.

Congress Should Strive to Differentiate

I think we know that there are ways that you cannot totally prevent, but substantially diminish, age-inappropriate uses through the Internet. That ought to be done here.

But I again want to repeat, and we're also told, "Well, gambling is this possible front for terrorism." Well, everything is a possible—everything. But there is zero evidence that we have, in fact, had people playing poker so they can bomb buildings. I await that evidence. I hope it isn't there. If it is, I'll look at it. But I don't believe it is.

I think, just to close, what we have is people who don't like gambling and think that they have a right, through the government, to prevent other people from doing it. I regard that as a very grave crossing of the line that we in government ought to respect.

*"The existence of government regulation
does not equate with security."*

Online Gambling Is Regulated
and Safe

Michelle Minton

*Michelle Minton is a policy analyst at the Competitive Enter-
prise Institute. In the following viewpoint, she states that anti-
online gambling advocates and politicians prey on the fears of
the public about online gambling when in fact gambling on the
Internet is safer in many respects than other forms of gambling.
Minton quells fears that online gambling is akin to the "Wild
West" and argues that it is not an exceptionally risky or corrupt
activity.*

As you read, consider the following questions:

1. According to Minton, what was the scandal surrounding
   the Internet payment service Neteller in 2007?

2. Who does Minton say is responsible for regulating online casinos?

3. What is the largest nongovernmental agency tasked with
   regulating online gambling, according to the viewpoint?

Michelle Minton, "The Truth About Online Gambling," *CEI On Point*, February 19,
2009. Copyright © 2009, CEI On Point. Reproduced by permission.

On Christmas morning 1869, in the dustbowl town of To-wash, Texas, the patrons of Jackie's Saloon heard the ringing of spurs against the wooden entrance steps and turned to see a tall man with a boyish face casually slide through the swinging doors. John Wesley Hardin, the 16-year-old son of a Confederate preacher, raised his gun with the grace of a portrait artist and painted the back wall of the bar with the blood of James Bradley—over a game of cards.

In the old West, this may have been a common way to ensure honesty at cards. Yet, as alien as that world seems to us today, some pundits and members of Congress suggest that things have not changed much since those gun-slinging days.

Today, gambling is legal in some form in all but two states and an overwhelming majority of Americans enjoy gambling—or have at least gambled once—and they do so in ever increasing numbers on the Internet. Dozens, if not hundreds, of websites let Americans place legal bets on everything from the spin of a virtual roulette wheel to the outcome of a horse race.

As the popularity of online gambling has grown, so too has the urge among some politicians and regulators who see it as a problem to "do something" about it. Fears about online gambling range from underage and problem gamblers accessing gaming sites to money laundering and threats to financial privacy.

Preying on Fears

Contrary to such fearmongering, recent examples of online gaming "scandals" have been isolated incidents, and are not symptomatic of a corrupt system. In fact, gambling on the Internet is safer in many respects than gambling in the real world.

Even so, such fears have resulted in repeated attempts to either limit or prohibit Americans' ability to gamble online, as some members of Congress portray Internet gambling as a lawless activity involving only cheats and victims. Most attempts by Congress over the past 10 years to limit or ban online gambling have been unsuccessful, but some recent high-profile scandals at gaming sites have revived such efforts.

- In 2008, employees of the popular online gambling platform Absolutepoker.com hacked the site's software and created "super-user" accounts that allowed them to cheat players out of millions of dollars over a two-year period before other players caught them.

- In 2007, the Internet payment service Neteller withheld millions in payments—almost all from gamblers—due to legal wrangling with the Department of Justice and the Internal Revenue Service and the arrest of some of its principals. The CEO [chief executive officer] eventually apologized and gamblers received their money back.

- In separate incidents, two websites, Betonsports.com and Hampton Casino, refused to pay out to winners of their games. Both cases were eventually settled.

- In the case of the London-based BetonSports, the company agreed to no longer serve U.S. customers. In 2003, Hampton Casino settled by paying the winner of a $1.3 million pot.

All of these scandals involved accusations of fraud that, if proven, would be punishable under a variety of existing laws in the United States and other countries. The question is not whether scandals can happen, but how society can best deal with them. A *60 Minutes* exposé of the Absolutepoker.com scandal explicitly compared online gambling to the "Wild West" and suggested that it exists outside of any effective regulation from governments, markets, or anybody else—and is illegal to boot. Certainly, online gambling may entail certain unique risks—one cannot hack the "software" of a *human* roulette dealer—but the evidence to date does not show that online gaming poses extraordinary risks to financial privacy.

With a few exceptions, gambling is legal in the United States. It is neither "unregulated" nor particularly vulnerable to cheaters. While online gambling carries risks, as does all gambling, it is not an exceptionally risky activity likely to be exploited by criminals. The corrupt or unscrupulous behavior of a few participants is not a valid basis for rebuking the entire industry. However, legislators often hold up these rare cases as evidence of widespread lawlessness and thus justification for laws that would ban or severally limit Americans' ability to gamble online.

Online Gambling Is Legal

Gambling online for money is legal in the United States, with some restrictions on sports betting discussed below. People who fall victim to fraud in online gambling operations are not lawbreakers. Internet gambling does not break any federal law and only one state in the union, Washington, expressly bans it for state residents. Three federal laws regulate Internet gambling.

- The [Interstate] Wire Act limits interstate transmission of sporting results for the purpose of betting.

- The Professional and Amateur Sports Protection Act (PASPA) bars certain states from legalizing sports gambling.

- The Unlawful Internet Gambling Enforcement Act (UIGEA) does not directly restrict gambling but instead deputizes banks, credit unions, and credit card companies to block illegal online gaming transactions.

None of these laws—and no state laws outside of Washington—bar individuals from placing non-sports bets online. Sports betting online, except on animal racing, is illegal everywhere except in states that offered any form of legal sports betting before PASPA passed in 1991. Almost all other online gambling is legal.

While UIGEA—which does not yet have implementing regulations in force—makes it illegal for banks and other credit processing companies to transfer money related to *unlawful* Internet wagering, it does not prohibit online gambling *per se*.

However, UIGEA's ambiguity—it lacks a definition for what constitutes "unlawful Internet gambling"—will create a *de facto* ban on Internet wagering in the United States when it goes into effect by making it prohibitively risky and expensive for credit processing agencies to determine what types of funds they can handle under the new law. To avoid risking fines or investigation, credit processing companies would simply refuse to handle any funds that could potentially be linked to unlawful gambling.

Internet Casinos Are Not Unregulated

While Internet gambling is less regulated than other industries in America—and less regulated in the U.S. than it is in Europe—reports of Internet gambling as a lawless "Wild West" are a far cry from reality. In reality, this multi-billion dollar industry is a well-oiled, well-maintained, and, for the most part, highly scrutinized entertainment platform.

As a result of gambling's unique development in America, there is no set federal regulator or official body tasked with overseeing online gambling. However, that does not mean that Internet gambling faces *no* government regulation. Many independently operated rating agencies offer certificates for sites that meet standards of security, legality (meaning they guarantee that age limits are strictly upheld), and fairness. Many of these rating organizations also require Internet casinos to participate in their dispute mediation services in the event that a

Online Poker Is Not as Dangerous as You Think

Opponents of online gambling focus on extreme cases and imply they're typical. A June 2007 hearing on Internet gambling held by the House Financial Services Committee featured testimony by an Ohio minister whose college-age son robbed a bank to pay off the debts he incurred while playing online poker. The research firm Ipsos estimates that 15 million Americans play online poker for money; most of them do not end up robbing banks. According to industry data collected by the Poker Players Alliance, the average online player spends $10 to $20 a week. Players like these are neither winning nor losing large amounts of money; they are mainly having fun, a concept that [Republican Congressman] Bob Goodlatte seems to have trouble comprehending.

Jacob Sullum, "Some Bets Are Off,"
Reason, May 18, 2008.

player feels cheated. These ratings are a viable and effective way for consumers to ensure that their rights are respected in the realm of online gaming.

All of the online casinos where Americans may play are physically housed in other countries (Costa Rica, Barbuda, and Antigua happily welcome online casinos). This means that they fall under the jurisdiction of those other countries, many of which do have some regulatory oversight of their activities. These sites' increasing popularity in the U.S. has increased the pressure for the American government to "do something" about online gambling, and created an incentive for new online casinos to keep their real-world addresses in other countries, thereby eschewing uncertain regulations.

Regulators come in two basic forms: government and private. The existence of government regulation does not equate with security. For example, the casino at the center of the Absolutepoker.com scandal fell under government regulation. Its regulator was the Kahnawake Gaming Commission, the regulatory body of the Kahnawake Mohawk Indian tribe in western Canada. Foreign governments directly regulate other casinos. England maintains its own system for regulating online gambling. Bermuda—well known for its strong financial regulation—is strongly considering creating a system similar to England's.

Nongovernmental agencies also regulate online gaming. The largest, eCogra, certifies over 100 sites for "fair gaming, player protection and responsible operator conduct." No one seems to have challenged eCogra's assertion that there has never been a scandal involving one of its certified sites. According to a recent joint study by eCogra and the European Gaming and Betting Association, comparing independent regulators to some of Europe's government-run regulatory regimes, independent organizations like eCogra did just as well, and 24 percent of the time independent regulators exceeded the standards of the government monopolies.

In short, a variety of regulators exist for online gambling and nearly all widely known sites submit to either a government regulator or a private agency like eCogra.

Cheating Online Is Hard

It is far easier to cheat in real-world casinos than it is online. Online cheating requires more technical skill, is easier to track, and is harder to get away with than cheating in the real world.

In the real world, cheating can take a variety of forms. For example, players can use marked cards, tamper with gambling devices, pay off dealers, move bets so they "pay off" in certain table games, stack a game with confederates, and employ other methods to otherwise goose the odds in their own favor. Most of these tactics are literally impossible to carry out in the virtual world.

To cheat at an online game, a player almost always needs to manipulate the software used to play the game. This is exactly what happened in the Absolutepoker.com scandal. Such inside jobs notwithstanding, many routes for cheating are closed to online players.

Cheating is also easier to track online. If a casino operator suspects that a player may be cheating, it is limited as to how much evidence it can collect—utilizing only dealer observation and video cameras. The "eye in the sky" (casino overhead camera) is only effective at watching players already suspected as cheaters and even then it is very difficult to use the video to actually prove that a player is cheating.

By comparison, it is far easier to spot, follow, and confirm cheating in online casinos by tracking all of the hands for a user attached to a certain IP [Internet protocol] address. In addition, Internet casino operators can write computer software to sound the alarm if pattern of play appears suspicious, even if no other player has noticed. And, unlike real-world casino operators, who can only monitor a player's activity in its own casino, Internet casinos can coordinate and track a user's IP address to monitor his activities across multiple Internet gaming platforms.

It Is Not the "Wild West"

Online gambling faces challenges common to any growing industry. Gambling online does, in many cases, imply unique threats and risks that do not apply in the "real" world—including computer viruses and adware. But online gambling is not illegal, does not take place in a lawless "Wild West" setting, and does not provide a particularly fertile ground for cheating. Those who gamble online need to be careful just as those who gamble in the real world need to be.

The market and rating agencies do an increasingly effective job of ensuring consumer safety. Those who want to make online gambling safer will do best to review the ways in which government interference in economic activity creates openings for unethical operators, rather than attempt to squash all activity. John Wesley Hardin is not lurking online.

| "Online gambling puts the equivalent of a casino—open all night, with no lines, waiting, age restrictions or regulations—in every American home."

Online Gambling Is Unregulated and Dangerous

John Shadegg

John Shadegg is a Republican congressman from Arizona. In the following viewpoint, he asserts that online gambling is particularly insidious because it is unregulated and Americans who indulge in it have no recourse if they are swindled. Shadegg also observes that because they are unregulated, the money gamblers spend can be funneled to organized crime, drug dealers, identity thieves, or even terrorist groups.

As you read, consider the following questions:

1. According to federal government studies, how much has the number of Internet gambling websites increased from 1998 to 2003?

2. According to *Sports Illustrated*, how much do online poker players wager on average every day?

John Shadegg, "Online Gambling Is Society's Issue," *Arizona Republic*, March 12, 2006. Reproduced by permission of the author.

3. According to the *NewsHour with Jim Lehrer*, what percentage of youths ages 10–17 gambled in 2006?

In December of last year [2005], Greg Hogan [Jr.] walked into a bank and handed the teller a note saying he had a weapon. The teller handed over nearly $3,000. The motive for the robbery? Hogan—the president of his sophomore class at Lehigh University, hardly the usual picture of a bank robber—had gotten deeply in debt by gambling online.

The Consequences of Online Gambling

I have seen how gambling can destroy families. In the late 1980s, I was working in the Arizona Attorney General's Office when state law was briefly changed to allow "social gambling" at neighborhood bars.

Law enforcement agencies statewide were flooded with phone calls, thousands of them, from wives and girlfriends whose husbands or live-in boyfriends had gambled away their paychecks.

I worked with officers from the Phoenix police vice squad who got these calls every week. The story they heard was always the same: The women, who almost always had children, were desperate. Their husband or boyfriend had gambled away his paycheck, usually for two or three weeks in a row, and the callers didn't know how they were going to pay the rent or put food on the table for the rest of the month.

The epidemic of unregulated online gambling affects families all over the country. Online gambling puts the equivalent of a casino—open all night, with no lines, waiting, age restrictions or regulations—in every American home.

Companies Find Loopholes

It is already against the law to use telephone lines for gambling. That was settled by the federal [Interstate] Wire Act in 1961. But as technology has changed, federal law has not kept

Online Gambling and Crime

Representatives of law enforcement agencies, regulatory bodies, and the credit card and gaming industries expressed mixed views regarding the vulnerability of Internet gambling to money laundering. Law enforcement officials said they believed that Internet gambling could potentially be a powerful vehicle for laundering criminal proceeds at the relatively obscure "layering" stage of money laundering. They cited several characteristics of Internet gambling that they believed made it vulnerable to money laundering, including the volume, speed, and international reach of Internet transactions and the offshore locations of Internet gambling sites. In their view, these characteristics promoted a high level of anonymity and gave rise to complex jurisdictional issues. Law enforcement officials acknowledged the lack of adjudicated cases involving money laundering through Internet gambling sites but cited what they believed to be contributing factors, including the lack of any industry regulations or oversight.

US General Accountability Office,
"Internet Gambling: An Overview of the Issues,"
December 2002.

up. Because it is not clear that the Wire Act applies to the Internet, online casinos and sports books are able to operate in the United States.

According to news accounts, in 2000, a bill to close this loophole and ban Internet gambling received 245 votes in the House of Representatives, a clear majority. But disgraced former lobbyist Jack Abramoff was able to have the legislation put on the "suspension calendar" so a two-thirds majority was necessary to pass it. As a result, it failed.

With Abramoff under indictment and facing prison, passing such legislation would be a sensible way for Congress to show it has put the era of improper lobbyist influence behind it.

According to federal government studies, from 1998 to 2003 the number of Internet gambling websites grew to 1,800 from 190. Online gambling revenue grew to $4.2 billion from $650 million over the same period. And these numbers are nearly three years old.

Big Money in Online Gambling

The sums of money involved in online gambling are huge. According to *Sports Illustrated*, online poker players wager an average of $200 million every day, and the industry generates more than $2.2 billion in gross revenue annually. That is just poker. Online sports books are an even bigger business, which is why every major professional sports league—Major League Baseball, the NFL [National Football League], NBA [National Basketball Association], NHL [National Hockey League]—and the NCAA [National Collegiate Athletic Association] support restricting online gambling.

Christiansen Capital Advisors [CCA], an investment firm that tracks the online gambling industry, estimates it is currently more than a $15 billion-a-year business. The industry is expected to continue to grow, and CCA projects that it will be nearly $25 billion by 2010.

Most importantly, online gambling is unregulated. When you walk into a casino, you have at least some hope there is a level of government oversight of the gaming rules. At state-regulated casinos, gamblers must be of legal age, and the odds of winning a game of chance are regulated.

None of that is ensured with online gambling. Americans who lose money to swindlers who operate an online casino have no effective recourse. The operations are mostly located offshore, and the owners of an online casino or sports book can be unknown.

Online Gambling Is a Shady Business

Online gamblers are giving out credit card numbers and other information with no idea where it will wind up. Online casinos can be fronts or money-laundering operations for organized crime, drug dealers, identity thieves or even terrorists. Even if you win at an online casino, there is a chance that you will never collect, and there is nothing you can do about it.

Make no mistake; gambling can lead to gambling addiction. The National Gambling Impact Study Commission found that, after a decade of casino expansion in the 1990s, the national population of lifetime compulsive gamblers had grown by at least 50 percent. It also discovered a significant trend indicating addiction had doubled in many populations within 50 miles of casinos. With Internet connections in most U.S. households, online gambling puts a casino right in your home.

As with other addictions, the earlier gambling addicts start, the worse problems they are likely to face. The *News-Hour with Jim Lehrer* reported last spring [2005] that more than 70 percent of youths ages 10 to 17 gambled in the past year [2006], up from 45 percent in 1988.

A study of America's 11- to 18-year-olds showed that 4 percent to 7 percent had demonstrated problem gambling behaviors. And mountains of debt and ruined credit are not the worst results. The National Council on Problem Gambling reports that one in five pathological gamblers attempts suicide, a rate higher than for any other addictive disorder.

Those who argue that gambling is a private matter that doesn't concern the government ignore that, as a society, we are all affected by the negative consequences of compulsive gambling.

Whether we like it or not, when gambling addicts neglect their families, taxpayers step in to provide the money for housing, food and health care. As a result, gambling, particularly unregulated, potentially corrupt gambling, is not a purely private matter. The government will help the victims, and we will all pay the consequences.

Internet gambling is a clear violation of the spirit and intent of our laws. We need to give law enforcement agencies every tool possible to crack down on the shadowy, illegal and dangerous world of Internet gambling; it is time to outlaw Internet gambling. Now.

"In fact, the real, the very real victims of illegal Internet gambling, the ones I'm concerned about, are the ones he spoke of, the underage gamblers who, by the tens of thousands, are becoming compulsive, addictive gamblers."

Online Gambling Creates Underage Gambling Addicts

Spencer Bachus

Spencer Bachus is a Republican congressman from Alabama. In the following viewpoint, he states that there is a serious epidemic of underage gamblers on the Internet, resulting in young people falling into debt and becoming drawn to crime and suicide. Bachus argues that Congress should be spending less time undermining the laws against online gambling and instead spending more time protecting America's youth, their families, and their communities from online gambling danger.

Spencer Bachus, "Can Internet Gambling Be Effectively Regulated to Protect Consumers and the Payment System?" Committee on Financial Services, US House of Representatives, June 8, 2007.

As you read, consider the following questions:

1. According to a study conducted by the University of Connecticut Health Center, what percentage of those who have used the Internet to gamble have serious, chronic problems with addiction?

2. According to a study by Harvard University, how many times more likely are teenagers to become addicted than adults?

3. What percentage of teen compulsive gamblers have attempted suicide, according to a study by McGill University?

One of the last acts that this Congress passed last year [2006] was the Unlawful Internet Gambling Enforcement Act. It passed 317 to 93, and enforcement of the act capped a multi-year effort to protect American families from the well-documented ill effects of illegal online gambling.

The new law attacks the problem of Internet gambling, illegal Internet gambling, through the payment systems, by prohibiting financial intermediaries from processing transactions involving unlawful gambling under applicable state and federal laws, including the Federal Wire Act [Interstate Wire Act], and the Professional and Amateur Sports Protection Act.

It does not prohibit anything which is not already illegal. It simply enforces the law that has existed in this country for years.

The Terrible Consequences of Gambling

As the record developed by this committee and the Judiciary Committee over the past several years has shown, gambling too often, illegal Internet gambling, results in addiction, bankruptcy, the destruction of families, and criminal activity. Internet gambling magnifies the destructiveness of gambling by bringing the casino into the home.

According to an extensive study conducted by the University of Connecticut Health Center, 74 percent of those who have used the Internet to gamble have serious, chronic problems with addiction, and many of those have resorted to criminal activities to pay for their habit.

One of the witnesses who is with us this morning, Pastor Greg Hogan, will share with this committee the story of how Internet gambling addiction placed his high-achiever son on a path that ultimately led to prison.

The NBA [National Basketball Association], the NCAA [National Collegiate Athletic Association], Major League Baseball, all of those testified before our committee as to the corrupting influence of illegal Internet gambling on athletes. Some claim that illegal Internet gambling is a victimless crime. The chairman has done that this morning.

The Real Victims

In fact, the real, the very real victims of illegal Internet gambling, the ones I'm concerned about, are the ones he spoke of, the underage gamblers who, by the tens of thousands, are becoming compulsive, addictive gamblers.

They can't go in a casino. They can't go in debt legally. So they do it on the Internet, which is prohibited and illegal, but they do it anyway. They do it in their bedrooms. They do it in their dorm rooms. It is a mushrooming epidemic, leaving in its wake suicides, crime, and financial and family tragedies.

The Judiciary Committee, and our committee, had several instances of college students who committed suicide as a result of Internet gambling and the debts they drove up. When it comes to illegal Internet gambling—and I stress, we're talking about illegal Internet gambling. So those who are testifying in favor of this bill are actually talking about taking away prohibitions on what is already illegal.

If the activity was legal, then it would have been in our court to try to make it illegal, but this is not a debate over

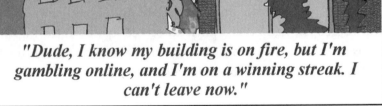

"Dude, I know my building is on fire, but I'm gambling online, and I'm on a winning streak. I can't leave now."

"Dude, I know my building is on fire, but I'm gambling online, and I'm on a winning streak. I can't leave now," cartoon by Jerry King. www.CartoonStock.com.

whether it's illegal or not. Every state in this union has a prohibition against this type of gambling.

Why Internet Gambling Is Dangerous

When it comes to this type of gambling, illegal Internet gambling, there are three reasons in particular why it is dangerous.

Number one, the Harvard Medical School, the University of South Florida, and the American Psychiatric Association all conducted studies showing that the earlier one begins gambling, the more likely it is he or she will become an addicted, problem gambler. In fact, the Harvard study—and you are a graduate of Harvard, Mr. Chairman—showed that teenagers are 3 or 4 times more likely to become addicted than the older population.

Second, preteens, teens, and college students have unlimited access to the Internet, 24 hours a day, 7 days a week. Because of the repeated exposure they have to illegal Internet sites, gambling sites, they fall victim by the thousands. These are illegal sites operated, most of them offshore, or all of them offshore, I would assume.

So the people who are operating these sites are violating the laws of our country. I don't know any other way to say it, other than that they are criminals. If you violate the criminal laws of our country, does that make you a criminal? I think it does. In fact, a University of Connecticut study showed that as many as three in four preteens and teens who are exposed to Internet gambling become addicted.

Third, compulsive, problem gambling, particularly among young people, has been shown to result in the following: Increased withdrawal from normal activities; and turning to criminal activities to recoup financial losses.

Rampant Gambling in the NCAA

The NCAA testified before the Judiciary Committee about the starting quarterback at Florida State University, who on an illegal Internet site ran up over $10,000 worth of debt, turned to burglary to try to solve this problem, was betting on games involving his own institution, and ended up in prison. He is only 1 of about 14 NCAA athletes who have been convicted in the past few years of illegal Internet gambling. A lot of people don't care about this. They make money on these games, they make money on these athletes, and so they aren't really concerned with whether the athletes end up in jail.

But this same study, the Connecticut study, showed that many of these teens turn to criminal activities to recoup their financial losses, they take drugs to deal with the depression, and as the Harvard study showed, the South Florida study, the American Psychiatric study, and 48 other studies by universities and health groups showed, their irresponsible behavior leads also to family and other relational problems.

A study by McGill University, and this is in the past 2 years—we didn't have the benefit of this study—found that nearly one-third of teen compulsive gamblers have attempted suicide.

The University of Pennsylvania has recently found that the number of young people addicted to gambling, largely due to what they found was an increased exposure to illegal Internet gambling, is growing by an alarming 20 percent between 2004 and late 2005.

They call this an epidemic which the country will deal with socially and economically for decades to come.

Congress Must Act

Thus, Congress's failure to act for many years, because of the resistance of many of the people pushing for today's bill, we are seeing the devastating consequences of efforts in this Congress for 2 or 3 years to stall our efforts.

The law we passed last year has already had a significant impact on the market for illegal gambling services, prompting the major players in the industry, many of which are publicly traded companies in the United Kingdom, to cease their U.S. operations immediately.

As reports in the *Washington Post* and others showed, they spent over $100 million resisting our effort to pass this bill. And yet, just as the new law is in the process of being implemented, through regulations that the Treasury and the Federal Reserve are expected to issue shortly, a concerted effort is already under way to undo it.

Congress Cannot Undermine the Law

Chairman [Barney] Frank has introduced legislation that we regulate rather than prevent gambling over the Internet. I don't question his motive, but the bill would establish the presumption in favor of legalized online casinos and sports betting—something that the NBA, Major League Baseball, the National Football League, and the NCAA worked for years to stop—and reward and legalize offshore Internet gambling sites that accept debts from Americans in violation of the U.S. law.

The licensing regime contemplated by the legislation is premised upon the ability of Internet gambling sites to detect and block attempts to gamble online by minors, compulsive gamblers, and individuals located in jurisdictions that legally prohibit gambling.

Let me say in conclusion, Mr. Chairman, that experts in the field of online protection and identity verification have openly questioned the effectiveness of technology currently available that attempts to verify age and identity in online settings, and advise the Judiciary Committee that only the prohibition we passed would work.

In summary, Mr. Chairman, there is no compelling reason to change the course that Congress wisely charted last year when it passed strong legislation to combat the scourge of Internet gambling.

Rather than spending our time trying to undermine the new law, we should be devoting our energies to rigorous implementation. America's youth, their families, and communities should expect no less.

| "Now, it is particularly interesting, and I call it ironic, that I am sitting here today saying that the only way to protect consumers from online gambling risks is by legalizing it."

Legalizing Online Gambling Will Protect Children and Teenagers

Parry Aftab

Parry Aftab is the executive director of WiredSafety, an Internet safety organization. In the following viewpoint, he contends that the only way to effectively protect consumers from the risks of online gambling is to legalize it, and then properly and strictly regulate it. Aftab recommends a holistic approach to the problem that includes not only regulating the financial aspects of online gambling, but also education, transparency, and security software tools.

As you read, consider the following questions:

1. According to the viewpoint, how many volunteers are part of WiredSafety?

Parry Aftab, "H.R. 2266, the Reasonable Prudence in Regulation Act; and H.R. 2267, the Internet Gambling Regulation, Consumer Protection, and Enforcement Act," Committee on Financial Services, US House of Representatives, December 3, 2009.

2. What was the name of the book Aftab wrote on Internet safety?

3. How can technology help protect children and teenagers, according to the author?

It is interesting as I have heard both opening statements, we agree at WiredSafety that children need to be protected. All of us are unpaid volunteers in a grassroots organization that is the world's largest and oldest Internet safety organization. I have about 16,000 volunteers in 76 countries around the world. We care desperately about the issues here. We act as an Internet safety organization and a help group dealing with all digital risks, all demographics and all digital technologies. We were appointed as one of the 29 members of the Internet Safety Technical Task Force that was run by the Berkman Center [for Internet & Society] at Harvard, and appointed to issue a report to 49 of the 50 state attorneys general, and I was recently appointed as one of the 24 members of the NTIA [National Telecommunications and Information Administration] working group on online safety that was commissioned to render a report to Congress in June of this coming year [2010] on child safety issues. We advise local and federal and state and international governmental agencies and nonprofits.

Recognizing the Problem of Online Gambling

Personally, I am an Internet privacy and security lawyer, but I haven't practiced law in a long time since creating the charity and donating my time to running it. In 1997, almost 13 years ago, I wrote the very first book on Internet safety for parents called *A Parent's Guide to the Internet*. My mother made me do it. It contained a chapter that dealt with online gambling. It was called, "Are We Raising Riverboat Gamblers?"

Three-and-a-half years after the launch of the web, we recognized that online gambling was a problem, something parents didn't understand and weren't sure how to deal with. In 1999, I wrote, *The Parent's Guide to Protecting Your Children in Cyberspace* for McGraw-Hill that also contained a chapter [dealing with online gambling], and it was replicated around the world as the book was rewritten and published in various jurisdictions.

Most people are aware of the moral arguments against gambling. A lot of people are aware of the regulatory and legal issues. Few of them understand that this really is a consumer protection problem. That is why I am at this table today. I have been following online gaming issues for a very long time. They affect not only children and parents, but there are people who are problem gamblers of all ages. We also have senior citizens who get online and may be scammed by rogue sites which take their money and make them promises and never pay on those bets. And I get e-mails; I get about 1,000 e-mails a day from people who come to us for help, and many of those are relating to online gambling.

Online Gambling Must Be Properly Regulated

Now, it is particularly interesting, and I call it ironic, that I am sitting here today saying that the only way to protect consumers from online gambling risks is by legalizing it. And I never thought I would ever say such a thing. But if we don't legalize it, we can't regulate it. And what I am finding now is that we are acting a bit like the "hear no evil, see no evil," and we have taken an approach that the only way to address online gambling, illegal online gambling, is by regulating the money systems, the financial systems. And I think that is an important piece of an entire puzzle, but the other pieces aren't there yet.

I think we need to . . . approach this from a holistic approach. We need to educate parents. We need to provide security software tools and parental control tools that are out there. Other countries are doing that. We need to make sure

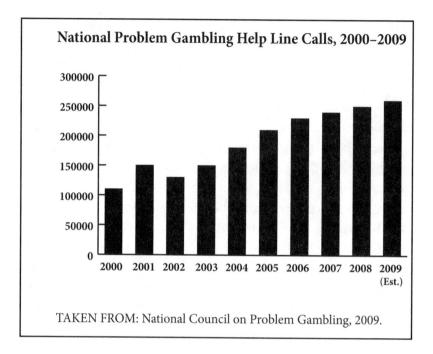

National Problem Gambling Help Line Calls, 2000–2009

TAKEN FROM: National Council on Problem Gambling, 2009.

that if online gambling sites are regulated and licensed, we know who they are, we know who is behind them. We can look to a lot of the brick-and-mortar regulatory schemes for making sure that we are dealing with trustworthy people, and their books are open so we know what money they are taking in and what money they are paying out to make sure that their processes are in place.

The Role of Technology

We can make sure that we teach the people who are gambling on these sites who are adults that use the latest technology to keep out everyone but adults. That means there may be some adults who aren't going to pass those screening tests, but it is a multilayer approach. And this technology has changed dramatically since the Children Online Protection Act case was first determined almost 3 years ago.

There are lots of different systems that you can put in place which, when combined, will keep most of the kids out.

Are they going to be able to keep a kid out if their father has opened up their online gambling account and forgot to close it off? Probably not, unless we put a system in place that closes that after the end of 15 minutes. Nothing is perfect, but whatever we do is better than what we have now.

We need to make sure that these sites are also using the latest methods to keep out malware and spyware, and that they are protecting our data and the personal information that is being given to them.

I do not advocate gambling anywhere; I advocate the protection of consumers and families and children. Representative [Spencer] Bachus and I are in full alignment, and I have many volunteers in his jurisdiction. We spend a great deal of time protecting children. As a citizen and a taxpayer, I would like us to have a tax, but that is not why I am here. I think that we can put something together if we take the great minds in this room and outside and come together with something that will be a holistic approach and will look to the rest.

Finding a Practical Approach

I thought these things would work. I have been working in this area for a long time trying to come up with practical approaches, but rather than putting my opinion out there, we commissioned a study. It was indeed paid for by gaming interests, but very carefully done so that no one controlled the results. I didn't, and neither did they. And we turned to one of the most respected law enforcement officials and academics ... at Harvard and asked him to look at existing regulatory schemes and look at all of the 10 risks that we identified and see if there is something outside of what I thought would work to put this together. You will be hearing from Mr. Sparrow shortly, and he can address those.

But I think, if working together, we can address these issues, all of our common concerns. We can make a difference. And perhaps the law that exists right now is an important part of that. I can't opine as to that. I can only tell you we need to do something, because whatever we have right now isn't enough.

Periodical and Internet Sources Bibliography

The following articles have been selected to supplement the diverse views presented in this chapter.

Larry Ashley	"Why Add More Options?" *New York Times*, July 29, 2010.
Radley Balko	"Bring Back Internet Gambling," *Reason*, June 11, 2007.
Alexandra Berzon	"Reid Backs Legalizing Poker," *Wall Street Journal*, December 3, 2010.
Annie Duke	"Personal Freedom," *New York Times*, July 29, 2010.
Christopher Flavelle	"Too Dangerous for College," *Newsweek*, August 26, 2009.
Earl L. Grinols	"Too Many Negative Side Effects," *New York Times*, July 29, 2010.
HealthDay	"Online Gambling Rises Among College Males, High School Girls," October 19, 2010. http://health.usnews.com.
Jeremy Herb	"High Stakes for Online Gamblers," *Newsweek*, November 20, 2009.
Sallie James	"Senator Reid's Gamble," *Cato@Liberty* (blog), December 8, 2010. www.cato-at-liberty.org.
Barry Meier	"Casinos Now See Online Gambling as a Better Bet," *New York Times*, October 3, 2010.
Jacob Sullum	"Some Bets Are Off," *Reason*, June 2008.
Walter E. Williams	"Truly Disgusting," Townhall.com, July 26, 2006. http://townhall.com.

For Further Discussion

Chapter 1

1. Should gambling be restricted in the United States? Read viewpoints by Les Bernal and Shikha Dalmia to inform your opinion.

2. Evan Weiner contends that sports betting should be legalized in more areas of the country. In her viewpoint, Diane M. Grassi argues that legalized sports betting has some major consequences, many of them negative. After reading both viewpoints, what is your opinion on sports betting? Would you welcome it in your hometown?

3. Several cities that allow dog racing are considering banning it. Read viewpoints by Amy Pedigo and the *Harvard Crimson*. Are you in favor of banning the sport? Why or why not?

4. In the past few years, life-ending injuries to several high-profile horses have put the sport of horse racing in the spotlight. After reading viewpoints by Jay Ambrose and Chris Antley, express your opinion on whether the sport should be banned, reformed, or left alone. Use information from the viewpoints to back up your opinion.

Chapter 2

1. For communities in dire financial straits, gambling looks like a sure way to bring in some much-needed revenue. Should policy makers depend on gambling for money? Why or why not? Read viewpoints by Nick Gillespie and Steven Malanga to inform your answer.

2. In a pair of viewpoints on racinos, Adam Ragusea argues that they hurt the economy and Gary Rotstein contends

that there are clear economic benefits. Which criteria do you believe should be more important when considering the issue of racinos?

Chapter 3

1. Thomas E. McClusky states that the federal ban on online gambling is warranted. Radley Balko, however, believes that the ban should be overturned. In a third viewpoint, Diane M. Grassi asserts that smarter legislation is needed when it comes to online gambling. After reading all three viewpoints, which do you think is more persuasive and why?

2. The 2005 World Trade Organization (WTO) decision on the US gambling ban was very controversial. Read about the decision in viewpoints by Phyllis Schlafly and Lorraine Woellert. Should the United States reject the WTO decision, as Schlafly suggests? Or should it honor its international commitments and heed the decision? In a larger sense, what jurisdiction should international organizations have in US affairs?

3. Should online poker be allowed in California? Robert Martin believes that it should be legal, but only with strict regulation. In her viewpoint, Michelle Minton argues that such restrictions would be "offensive to defenders of individual rights, open markets, or personal privacy." Read both views and provide your opinion on the matter.

Chapter 4

1. Online gambling opponents like Bob Goodlatte argue that the practice is harmful, particularly for college and high school students. Jacob Sullum, however, takes the view that the dangers have been sensationalized. Which perspective do you think is more persuasive? How harmful do you think online gambling is?

2. Do you think the government should be protecting citizens from the dangers of online gambling? Or should people have the freedom to make their own decision on the activity? Read viewpoints by Spencer Bachus and Barney Frank to inform your answer.

3. Michelle Minton states in her viewpoint that online gambling is regulated and safe. John Shadegg counters that view by arguing that it is largely unregulated and dangerous. Which viewpoint presents more clear and persuasive evidence to support her or his assertion?

4. The consequences of online gambling, especially for pathological gamblers, have long been a concern to opponents of the practice. In his viewpoint, Spencer Bachus lays out the case that online gambling creates underage gambling addicts. Conversely, Parry Aftab argues that legalizing online gambling will actually help *protect* children and teenagers. In your opinion, how do we best protect young people from becoming pathological gamblers? Defend your view.

Organizations to Contact

The editors have compiled the following list of organizations concerned with the issues debated in this book. The descriptions are derived from materials provided by the organizations. All have publications or information available for interested readers. The list was compiled on the date of publication of the present volume; names, addresses, phone and fax numbers, and e-mail and Internet addresses may change. Be aware that many organizations take several weeks or longer to respond to inquiries, so allow as much time as possible.

American Gaming Association (AGA)
1299 Pennsylvania Avenue NW, Suite 1175
Washington, DC   20004
(202) 552-2675 • fax: (202) 552-2676
e-mail: info@americangaming.org
website: www.americangaming.org

The American Gaming Association (AGA) is an advocacy organization for the American gaming entertainment industry. The AGA works to promote the interests of the industry by disseminating facts to the public, media, legislators, and policy makers and lobbying lawmakers for fair laws and regulations. The AGA publishes a number of resources to educate the public, including *Responsible Gaming Quarterly*, which is a joint newsletter of the AGA and the National Center for Responsible Gaming (NCRG). The AGA website features an e-store, which offers a wide range of industry-related research and studies.

Gamblers Anonymous
PO Box 17173, Los Angeles, CA   90017
(213) 386-8789 • fax: (213) 386-0030
e-mail: isomain@gamblersanonymous.org
website: www.gamblersanonymous.org

Gamblers Anonymous is a support group and recovery program for problem gamblers. It is described on its website as "a fellowship of men and women who share their experience, strength and hope with each other that they may solve their common problem and help others to recover from a gambling problem." The organization's website provides information on gambling addictions and offers a list of Gamblers Anonymous meetings throughout the United States and in a number of other countries.

Greyhound Racing Association of America (GRA/America)
110 W. Ninth Street #813, Wilmington, DE   19801
(800) 372-3047 • fax: (443) 946-0683
website: www.gra-america.org

The Greyhound Racing Association of America (GRA/America) is a nonprofit membership organization that is devoted to improving the reputation of greyhound racing in the United States "through positive media exposure and responsible greyhound ownership." The GRA/America website has a list of active greyhound racetracks; outlines the rules and regulations of the sport; links to other greyhound and greyhound racing associations; and offers information on the Greyhound Hall of Fame. It also posts articles of interests, press releases, and information on recent events.

Interactive Gaming Council (IGC)
175-2906 West Broadway, Vancouver, BC   V6K 2G8
    Canada
(604) 732-3833 • fax: (604) 677-5785
website: www.igcouncil.org

The Interactive Gaming Council (IGC) is a worldwide, nonprofit membership organization formed to advance the interests of the global gaming entertainment industry. It also functions as an information clearinghouse and public advocate for gaming interests. One of the key roles of the IGC is to establish fair and responsible trade guidelines and practices that inspire confidence among consumers, regulators, and policy makers. These guidelines can be viewed on the IGC website, which also features a calendar of events for industry players. In addition, recent articles of interest on a variety of industry issues are posted on the website. The IGC's Helping Hand program offers assistance for individuals who are problem gamblers and educates beginners on responsible gaming.

National Center for Responsible Gaming (NCRG)
1299 Pennsylvania Avenue NW, Suite 1175
Washington, DC   20004
(202) 552-2689 • fax: (202) 552-2676
e-mail: info@ncrg.org
website: www.ncrg.org

The National Center for Responsible Gaming (NCRG) is a national association that works to fund research on pathological and youth gambling and to raise awareness about responsible gaming practices. The NCRG finds and supports effective treatment options for those with gambling addictions. The NCRG's Research Center offers the latest research studies on pathological gambling, youth gambling, and other disorders and can be found on the group's website. NCRG publishes *Responsible Gaming Quarterly* in collaboration with the American Gaming Association (AGA), as well as *The Wager*, a monthly review of the latest scientific research on gambling disorders.

National Council on Problem Gambling (NCPG)
730 Eleventh Street NW, Suite 601, Washington, DC   20001
(202) 547-9204 • fax: (202) 547-9206
e-mail: ncpg@ncpgambling.org
website: www.ncpgambling.org

The National Council on Problem Gambling (NCPG) is a nonprofit and independent organization that advocates for pathological gamblers and their families. The NCPG states that its mission is "to increase public awareness of pathological gambling, ensure the widespread availability of treatment for problem gamblers and their families, and to encourage research and programs for prevention and education." NCPG operates the National Problem Gambling Helpline Network, which is a number problem gamblers can call to get access to local resources. It hosts the National Conference on Problem Gambling and organizes the National Problem Gambling Awareness Week.

National Indian Gaming Association (NIGA)
224 Second Street SE, Washington, DC   20003
(202) 546-7711 • fax: (202) 546-1755
e-mail: questions@indiangaming.org
website: www.indiangaming.org

Founded in 1985, the National Indian Gaming Association (NIGA) is a nonprofit organization representing Native American people and businesses engaged in the American gaming entertainment industry. NIGA is devoted to providing economic, political, and social opportunities for Native American groups. It also offers "a clearinghouse and education, legislative and public policy resources for tribes, policy makers and the public on Indian gaming issues and tribal community development." The NIGA website presents a wide range of educational and training materials, including handbooks, training manuals, maps, brochures, research directories, and economic analyses.

National Thoroughbred Racing Association (NTRA)
2525 Harrodsburg Road, Suite 400, Lexington, KY   40504
(800) 792-6872
e-mail: ntra@ntra.com
website: www.ntra.com

The National Thoroughbred Racing Association (NTRA) is a coalition of groups involved in the sport of horse racing, including thoroughbred racetrack management, owners, breeders, trainers, and affiliated horse racing associations that are working to promote the sport and increase its popularity in America. The NTRA is also tasked with improving the economics of horse racing for its members. The NTRA website features schedules of thoroughbred horse racing events, videos of recent races, and clips of the latest racing news. It also has available podcasts, blogs, and teleconferences.

Stop Predatory Gambling Foundation
100 Maryland Avenue NE, Room 310
Washington, DC   20002
(202) 567-6996
e-mail: mail@stoppredatorygambling.org
website: stoppredatorygambling.org

The Stop Predatory Gambling Foundation is a coalition of antigambling groups formed to stop predatory gambling. One of the main ways it works to accomplish its mission is to educate the media, individuals, and policy makers on the consequences of gambling. To this end, the foundation conducts and disseminates research to support that position; much of this research can be found on its website. The foundation is also developing a curriculum for teachers to inform their students of the dangers of gambling. The website hosts a blog that covers recent events and breaking news, and it also features videos and photos.

World Trade Organization (WTO)
Centre William Rappard, Rue de Lausanne 154
Geneva 21   CH-1211
   Switzerland
(41-22) 739 51 11 • fax: (41-22) 739 42 06
e-mail: enquiries@wto.org
website: www.wto.org

Established in 1995, the World Trade Organization (WTO) is an international organization tasked with the responsibility of negotiating and regulating trade between nations to ensure fair global trade in a range of products and services. The WTO works to lower trade barriers between countries, mediates trade disputes, monitors the global trading system, facilitates binding trade agreements, and aims to improve the quality of life for its member countries. The WTO researches and publishes a variety of statistical analyses on international trade, in-depth reports, and studies such as the *World Trade Report*, an annual publication that examines trading trends and relevant trade issues. Seminars and speeches are webcast on the WTO website and are available for podcast. A special forum for students on the website provides basic and detailed information on the organization.

Bibliography of Books

Christine Adamec *Pathological Gambling.* New York:
Chelsea House, 2010.

Peter J. Adams *Gambling, Freedom and Democracy.*
New York: Routledge, 2008.

Steve Budin with *Bets, Drugs, and Rock & Roll: The*
Bob Schaller *Rise and Fall of the World's First*
Offshore Sports Gambling Empire.
New York: Skyhorse Publishing, 2007.

Sean Clancy *Barbaro: The Horse Who Captured*
America's Heart. Lexington, KY:
Eclipse Press, 2007.

Billye B. Currie *The Gambler: Romancing Lady Luck.*
Toronto: Inner City Books, 2007.

Diane Rae Davis *Taking Back Your Life: Women and*
Problem Gambling. Center City, MN:
Hazelden, 2009.

Charlotte *Pathways to Excessive Gambling: A*
Fabiansson *Societal Perspective on Youth and*
Adult Gambling Pursuits. Burlington,
VT: Ashgate, 2010.

Richard Hoffer *Jackpot Nation: Rambling and*
Gambling Across Our Landscape of
Luck. New York: HarperCollins, 2007.

Michael Konik *The Smart Money: How the World's*
Best Sports Bettors Beat the Bookies
Out of Millions: A Memoir. New York:
Simon & Schuster, 2006.

Marilyn Lancelot   *Gripped by Gambling.* Tucson, AZ: Wheatmark, 2007.

Jason W. Lee and   *Sport and Criminal Behavior.*
Jeffrey C. Lee,   Durham, NC: Carolina Academic
eds.   Press, 2009.

Richard A.   *The Gambling Debate.* Westport, CT:
McGowan   Greenwood Press, 2008.

Edward A. Morse   *Governing Fortune: Casino Gambling*
and Ernest P.   *in America.* Ann Arbor: University of
Goss, eds.   Michigan Press, 2007.

Laurence S. Moss,   *Perspectives on Gambling: Lotteries,*
ed.   *Wagers, and Casinos.* Malden, MA:
    Blackwell, 2007.

Jim Orford   *An Unsafe Bet?: The Dangerous Rise*
    of Gambling and the Debate We
    Should Be Having. Malden, MA: John
    Wiley & Sons, 2010.

Ryan H. Reed   *Born to Run: The Racing Greyhound*
    from Competitor to Companion.
    Lexington, KY: Thoroughbred Times
    Books, 2010.

Chris Roberts   *Casinos: Organizations and Culture.*
and Kathyrn   Boston: Prentice Hall, 2010.
Hashimoto

Paul Ruschmann   *Legalized Gambling.* New York:
    Chelsea House, 2009.

David G.   *Roll the Bones: The History of*
Schwartz   *Gambling.* New York: Gotham Books,
    2006.

Todd E.
Simmons, ed.

Regulating Internet Gambling. New
York: Nova Science Publishers, 2009.

Sam Skolnik

*High Stakes: The Rising Cost of
America's Gambling Addiction.*
Boston: Beacon Press, 2011.

Mary Sojourner

*She Bets Her Life: A True Story of
Gambling Addiction.* Berkeley, CA:
Seal Press, 2010.

Cameron L.
Stratton, ed.

*Thoroughbred Horseracing and the
Welfare of the Thoroughbred.* New
York: Nova Science Publishers, 2009.

Matti Viren, ed.

*Gaming in the New Market
Environment.* New York: Palgrave
Macmillan, 2008.

Douglas M.
Walker

The Economics of Casino Gambling.
New York: Springer, 2007.

Index